BREEDING &
SHOWING
Purebred Dogs
More Adventures on the
Road to Westminster

Other books by Robert B. and Toni C. Freeman:

The Road to Westminster: How to Select and Train a Purebred Dog and Prepare it for the Show Ring

BREEDING & SHOWING
Purebred Dogs

More Adventures on the Road to **Westminster**

Robert B. Freeman & Toni C. Freeman

BETTERWAY BOOKS
Cincinnati, Ohio

Cover design by Rick Britton
Cover photograph by Helen Boyer
Photographs by Robert and Toni Freeman
Typography by Kurt H. Fischer

Breeding and Showing Purebred Dogs. Copyright 1992 © by Robert B. Freeman and Toni C. Freeman. Printed and bound in the United States of America. All rights reserved. No part of this book may be reproduced in any form or by any electronic or mechanical means including information storage and retrieval systems without permission in writing from the publisher, except by a reviewer, who may quote brief passages in a review. Published by Betterway Books, an imprint of F&W Publications, Inc., 1507 Dana Avenue, Cincinnati, Ohio 45207. 1-800-289-0963. First edition.

96 95 94 93 92   5 4 3 2

Library of Congress Cataloging-in-Publication Data
Freeman, Robert B.
  Breeding and showing purebred dogs: more adventures on the
  road to Westminster / Robert B. Freeman and Toni C. Freeman.
    p. cm.
  Includes index.
  ISBN 1-55870-227-X (paperback): $8.95
  1. Dogs -- Breeding. 2. Dog shows. I. Freeman, Toni C.
II. Title
SF427.2F74 1992
                                                    91-43801
636.7'088.8' -- dc20   CIP

In Loving Memory
of
Coventry's Danny Boy

Portrait by Jack Helman

Never a blue ribbon or a trophy, but Danny won the hearts of all who knew him. Nursemaid to puppies, the clown who made us laugh, the very best kitty washer in history, our dearest friend. We can only hope they give lots of cookies in heaven.

Acknowledgments

We wish to express gratitude to the following for their contributions to this volume:

All Clumber Spaniels who ever lived;
Every other breed of dog, past and present;
Ron and Louise Larsen, breeders of our first Clumber;
Bill and Sandy Blakeley, our mentors;
James A. Boatman, V.M.D., for many years of compassionate animal care;
The Altoona Area Kennel Club, for continuing support;
James W. Takacs, V.M.D., reviewer of all things medical;
The Weekend Warriors, from whom we continue to learn;
The Judges and A.K.C., without whom and which we would have to blame ourselves; and
Kathy Zalewski, our borrowed handler, helper, kid.

Preface

We have returned. Those of you who walked the Road with us through *The Road to Westminster: How to Select and Train a Purebred Dog and Prepare It for the Show Ring* know that we befriended an imaginary puppy buyer, Lynnedora. Since she and her family were interested in the sport of dogs as a family recreation, we took them from the purchase of a puppy, which she named Throckmortana, an equally imaginary Clumber Spaniel bitch, to the Best-of-Breed competition at an all-breed show.

There were raised eyebrows! Why a Clumber Spaniel—a rare breed —rather than German Shepherd dogs or Golden Retrievers? We chose a Clumber because we love, breed, and compete them. Our data bank on Clumbers runneth over. Since we attempted to generalize the information offered and avoid breed-specific references, it makes very little difference what breed we use as an example.

In any event, after helping Lynnedora — and others, we hope — from puppy-proofing the facility to ring readiness, we took our leave. Except for a phone call here and there to iron out little kinks, Lynnedora, Throck, and family no longer needed us. They traveled, photographed, competed, and enjoyed.

Before we left them to realize the fruits of their many labors and practice sessions, however, we promised Lynnedora that, should Throck win her Championship, and animal and people maintain their enthusiasm for the sport, we would again make ourselves available to them if they ever decided to embark on a breeding program or contemplated campaigning a Champion.

Everyone who considers breeding needs help getting started whether they realize it or not. We certainly did. Breeding purebreds is literally a subject of life and death. There are many questions to be answered, such as who, what, and when? Where, why, and how? There are many weighty topics to discuss and much soul searching to do.

And if we extend ourselves to accept the responsibilities of breeding, do we also immerse ourselves in the advanced levels of competition, such as group placements or Best-in-Show? Should we campaign? What is involved in that? Specialties and international competition? Where does it all end?

Veterans of the sport will tell you it never ends. As far as we are concerned, the ultimate in competition — the brass ring so to speak — is a Best-in-Show victory at Westminster. One brief, shining moment before starting over again.

Well, Throckmortana won her championship. Lynnedora and her still-enthusiastic family contacted us immediately. Thus this new book, *Breeding and Showing Purebred Dogs: More Adventures on the Road to Westminster.*

If you, too, entertain thoughts of breeding purebred dogs or are wandering in search of the elusive brass ring (perhaps both), join us. We cannot promise Lynnedora or our readers that they will ever breed the superior animal in their breed of choice, but we can prepare you for the trials and tribulations you will encounter while trying. Nor can we promise any of you the ultimate victory, but we can explain how to play the game.

Contents

SECTION I — BREEDING

SECTION II — THE BIG TIME

I

BREEDING

1.

Improving the Breed

When we heard Lynnedora's voice on the line, we suspected good news. Though it had been a while since we last spoke with her or any of her family, we faithfully checked each monthly issue of the invaluable American Kennel Club publication *Show Awards* and thus had followed Throckmortana's progress, championship point by championship point, major by major. (Those familiar with the sport and/or readers of *The Road to Westminster* know that fifteen points, including two majors under two different judges, must be accomplished for a purebred to become a Champion.) At our last count, Throckmortana held thirteen points and her two majors. Only two points to go.

Lynnedora's tone, somewhere between euphoria and hysteria, erased all doubt as to the reason for her call. "We did it!" she shouted into the phone. "Throck is now Champion Rose Runs Throckmortana!"

What memories this news forced from our archives. Too many years ago, we had placed a similar call to the breeders of Christina, our first Clumber bitch. We can only hope that those good people took as much pleasure from our success as we did from Lynnedora's and Throckmortana's. Those veterans who are no longer affected by such enthusiasm from beginners have probably been in the sport too long.

About the fourth or fifth time through, Lynnedora calmed down long enough to ask if we would still be willing to help them advance to the next plateau. Both Throckmortana and her human family loved the sport, she assured us. Now she wanted us to help plan a program that would allow them to continue in the sport and experience new dimensions.

No argument from us. The sport, at all levels, can always use new blood. What better addition than a family doing it together.

WHY DO YOU WANT TO BREED? _____

"What we really want to do is breed our own Clumbers."

We looked at each other for a moment. They want to be breeders. That's what we are — breeders, with many years of experience, years of smiles and tears. Would we still elect to breed if we had it all to do again? We certainly have no regrets, but still, maybe we would not do it again! An excited young family with a new Champion would not understand that. Almost in unison we asked *why* they wanted to breed. An elementary question, but there are right answers and wrong answers.

"To help improve the breed. We want to breed strong, healthy Clumbers that are competitive in conformation, obedience, the field, or all three."

Just the answer we want to hear. She could have replied that Clumbers, being a rare breed, command a somewhat higher puppy price than more popular breeds. With good management and several litters a year, breeding could become a profitable business.

We are glad she did not respond that way. It would have been the wrong answer and a misguided answer. Responsible breeders seldom, if ever, make a profit. Only indiscriminate, puppy-mill breeding could ever bring enough profit to interest anyone, and that is at the expense of the animals. For most of us, whether involved with race or popular breeds, a glorious year would be that in which we break even.

Almost lacking as much merit is the response, often heard from gushing parents, that they want to share the beauty of the birth miracle with their children. There is very little miracle involved and the process is often as ugly as it is beautiful. The other half of birth is death. Unless you are anxious to expose them to both, do not expose your children to the whelping.

Every year there are thousands of purposeless or ill-purposed animal breedings. Humane Societies and like organizations destroy millions of dogs, cats, and other animals each year. Not purebreds, you say? Wrong! Purebreds constitute an alarmingly high percentage of the horrifying total.

Lynnedora, true to form, did not offer either of those two answers or variations thereof. As usual, Lynnedora's response and attitude pleased us. As a result, we invited her and her husband to join us to overview the possibility. At the same time, since our initial conversation might not be everything they wanted to hear, we suggested they leave the children home.

Two days later Lynnedora and her husband kept their appointment. As a special bonus they hauled along Throck and the young male we had loaned to their children for Junior Handling. Happy days are when you get to hug your kids and in return receive a tongue wash.

TO BREED OR NOT TO BREED _____

"Will you try to discourage us from breeding?"

We have no such intention. Nor do we intend to encourage you irresponsibly. What we really hope to do is to acquaint you with the bad and the good, then allow you to make a more informed decision as to whether or not you desire to continue. We could not think of anyone we would rather have join us and the other breeders, if that is what you really want. On the other hand, we would feel very bad if we allow you to commit time, money, and emotion without some early warnings. Far, far, far too often we see such excursions end in disaster for people and animals. It is better to test a friendship and turn aside a potential breeder than to launch a nice family into something they cannot handle.

We are very serious about this. Breeding, although largely a crap-shoot, is not a game. Living things are involved — breeders, the bred dogs, and the puppies. A good breeding program takes them all into consideration.

Expenses

Let's talk about the expense, for example. A breeding program includes the puppies, the young and coming breeding stock, breedable bitches, studs, and geriatrics (older dogs past the breeding stage). Redoing your facility to accommodate and separate all of those categories requires a sizeable investment. A dozen or so animals can boost your food bill to two or three hundred dollars a month. Imagine the cost of shots and other veterinary bills. Now add the cost of putting Championships on those you breed.

True, you will, if all goes well, produce puppies that you can sell. But only years of involvement and considerable good luck will ever bring you to a financial position that resembles a balanced budget.

And we do not even assign a monetary value to time in these calculations. Believe us when we tell you that your time involvement increases geometrically, not arithmetically, with the addition of each animal.

Other Necessities

Your family will have to consider forsaking other pleasures for the animals. Clumbers, for example, are primarily white. Think how much time must be spent bathing and hosing them when the world turns to rain and mud. Who will watch the kennel when the family is off to one of those two-, three-, or four-day show circuits?

Please do not forget love and affection. A breeder may soon have a dozen or more animals that want to both give and receive love and affection. Each wants to know the pride of walking on lead with Mom or Dad, to fetch that ball, to lie on that lap. Where do you find the time to accept all that they want to give and to give what they need in return?

"It sounds like we have a whole lot of family thinking and talking to do."

Death

While you're thinking and talking, devote a chunk of time to a consideration of how well the family can handle death. The sadness of parting with a sold puppy, a puppy you may well see again, is one thing. The sadness of burying puppies born dead, puppies who fade during the first few days, or mothers who develop problems is quite a different thing.

At least it is for most people, but not for all people. We hear tales of the legendary German breeders who, at times, destroy entire litters because the puppies do not meet expectations. There are most assuredly breeders in the U.S. who cull large litters of fourteen, sixteen, or eighteen puppies by destroying what they consider to be the bottom half in quality. We cannot destroy a healthy puppy, but there are those who can and will "for the good of the breed."

These are tough mental images to wrestle with, but it is an exercise that every reader who wants to understand breeding must endure. Enjoy your pictures of the bright side — new lives, healthy puppies bounding across the floor in pursuit of shoelaces, adult animals that can favorably impact the breed. But to do so while ignoring the other side — the pain and tears — is to indulge in a dangerous fantasy.

An example is appropriate here. As I sat down to pen the words of our first book, *The Road to Westminster*, we had a nine-month-old Clumber girl by the name of Sara living with us. Her picture, with that of her littermates, appears on the cover of that book. Perhaps, to the untrained eye, Sara appeared normal. And in many ways she was. Sara recognized her name, enjoyed affection, loved cookies, and tried to come when she was called.

Tried to come. She also tried to stand when she urinated or defecated. But Sara was born with cerebral damage and was prone to seizures. Her back legs most often failed to receive the messages she sent them. Much of the time she dragged her rear assembly because she could not elevate it, or her legs failed and she crashed to the ground.

Many breeders would have put her down with the first head tremor — at the least after the first seizure. But a respected vet offered hope that she might outgrow the worst of the malady. We chose to let her live as long as there was a chance she could possibly have a life of quality, even if she would be different from the rest of our animals.

We also had a six-week-old puppy, Tiny-Tiny. She played and wrestled and hollered for food. And she demonstrated the same early symptoms of cerebral damage that Sara did.

Neither Sara nor Tiny-Tiny was in physical pain, not apparently at any rate. The hope for them both was that they might outgrow the tendency to have seizures and learn to function well enough to enjoy an acceptable quality of life. The prospects for that happy conclusion soon dimmed with Sara. And there was no reason to hope for more with Tiny-Tiny. Though it tore our hearts to shreds, we forced ourselves to the dreaded decision and had them put to sleep. Both of these little girls are now at peace in puppy heaven.

THE DECISION

Before you decide to become a breeder, ask yourself if you could take those two loving puppies to your vet and have them put down. In the long run, to do so is a kindness, saving them from a life of unending struggle and severely limited quality. In the short run, it is the termination of little beings that trustingly climbed into your arms to go for their last ride.

Before you decide whether you could or could not do so, remember that the litters that brought the agony of Sara and Tiny-Tiny also provided us with beautiful, healthy pups. This too is part of breeding.

It is a lot to think about. We hope that many of you will continue through the pages of this book and become conscientious and dedicated breeders. We need you.

Consider the above and think carefully. If you decide you are presently too fragile to handle strain and sorrow, that the time requirements and expenditures imposed by a breeding program are beyond you at the moment, set this volume on the shelf for another time. Those who consider carefully and decide they are ready need only pick up the book again. We are waiting for you on the next page.

2.

A Maximum Breeding
Program

"We took our time," Lynnedora said when she called, "and had several serious discussions." She hesitated and took a deep breath. "Our family believes the rewards justify the sorrows. But —" Another long pause.

"Could we go through the whole thing with you, in detail? You know us. If we start, we will go the whole way. Before we plunge in, we would like to be absolutely sure of what breeding requires. Is that reasonable?"

"Ready! Where do we start?"

At the beginning, of course. We wish to present two scenarios. In this chapter, we want to describe what we consider to be the full-scale, maximum breeding program that could be accomplished by a family without hiring outside help.

In the next chapter, we will describe a more conservative approach for those with more limited time, facilities, and finances, and then discuss the first steps in breeding for either plan. Even those with the assets and wherewithal to accomplish the maximum program may wish to take the modified tack. We understand that thinking, because we chose that direction and moved one step at a time.

In either event, our hope is that we save you some of the false starts and wrong decisions that we suffered during our early years.

SETTING UP A BREEDING PROGRAM_____

Because of the great diversity in breeds, differences in existing facilities, variables in climate, and other factors, we can only generalize on the topic of facility upgrade. Before we can offer those generalizations, however, we must first arrive at an estimate of how large a population we must provide facilities for.

Short of becoming a puppy mill, a breeder will probably never have occasion to breed more than three litters a year. A litter is a lot of work.

And, as with Clumbers, we usually hold what we believe to be show grade puppies until four months plus. Even if the litters come at perfect intervals, which they will not, there is still an overlap.

"Do we have to have three litters a year to be good breeders?"

A good breeder does what he is capable of doing well. Remember that we are discussing maximums here. The individual must modify accordingly. If all the breeder can handle is one litter every other year, then that is the correct program. For those who would exceed our maximums, we wish you success — and a large family, many friends, or the funds to hire help.

"Three litters a year. How large would our population be at any given moment?"

That is not an easy question to answer because much depends on certain policy decisions the breeder must make. We will not, however, leave the question dangling. Since Lynnedora has a quality bitch already, we can start with bitches and calculate the population necessary for a full-scale breeding program.

We do not consider breeding a bitch until she is at least two years old. There was a time when we might have said we would not consider breeding a bitch until she was two years old and had her Championship. The latter part is all well and good and looks nice on the pedigree. But it is also very costly and not really necessary to put Championships on all your breeding stock.

The reason people wanted those Championships in the past was because, in theory, the judges awarded victories and Championships to those animals most suited to be reproduced as typical of the breed. That criterion does not appear to be quite as valid as it once was. Many current judges make questionable evaluations in that area. Not every Champion is indeed worthy of being reproduced, nor should you hesitate to breed worthy non-Champions.

As a breeder, you must learn to recognize excellence in your breed. If your bitch, for example, loves shows, take her and win. If she hates them, breed an excellent bitch without the Championship. Except for a few very particular show-quality buyers, most of your customers will never even ask if the puppy is from Champions.

Breeding Schedules

Breed a bitch at two years or later. The bitches appear to profit physically from a rest between litters. We take their need for rest seriously, asking no more than two litters per bitch in a lifetime, three at the very most. Litters from the same bitch are never closer than a year apart, and the bitch is spayed at six years old. Quick math tells you the bitch's productive life is four years long. During that time, say at two and four or three and five, she will give you her two litters. If she has a very easy time, adds good traits to the pups, and stays healthy, maybe a third litter can be considered. In that case there would be a litter when she is two, four, and six.

If Lynnedora wants to go full capacity the first year, she would need to go out and buy at least three two-year-old bitches to group with Throck, although she projects only three litters a year. The extra bitch is insurance. If Lynnedora breeds a bitch that does not conceive, it could be eight months before the bitch cycles again. An eight-month wait on a bitch that didn't conceive in June would carry into the following year and defeat the three litters a year schedule. Rather than wait, Lynnedora can breed the bitch she bought for insurance against such delays and keep her breeding program on track.

That is not to say that the purchase of an insurance bitch mitigates all the scheduling problems. It does not. Maintaining a breeding schedule can provide complexities that tend to elevate the frustration levels. Say, for example, that Lynnedora breeds Throck, whom we shall refer to as Bitch A. Lynnedora waits four weeks, then takes Throck to the vet for palpation and the assurance that there are puppies. (Caution! Those of you who read about Christina in *The Road to Westminster* recall that a litter is never a certainty, even given the assurances of the vet, until the breeder sees the pups squirming in the whelping box and hears them demanding food.)

The scenario probably sounds neither very complex nor very frustrating to this point. Stay with us. While Lynnedora was waiting the four weeks to take Bitch A to the vet, Bitch B came into season. If Lynnedora decides against breeding Bitch B, only to discover that Bitch A has not conceived, she misses both opportunities and watches her plan for three litters that year evaporate. The obvious alternative is for Lynnedora to breed Bitch B as well as Bitch A. If one does not conceive and the other does, Lynnedora takes credit for a good decision. But what if both bitches conceive? Lynnedora makes the wrong decision. Properly raising two litters at the same time is more work than a breeder should have to endure.

We can make it still more complicated. Let us say that in this particular year there are three superior stud dogs available—X, Y, and Z. Lynnedora does the necessary research and calculates that X is the perfect mate for Bitch A, Y for Bitch C, and Z for Bitch D. There is also a stud dog called Melvin, an outcross for all but B and an average-at-best caliber male. When Lynnedora options to breed Bitch B, just in case, she finds she can only use Melvin on her. She is thus not only saddled with two litters at the same time, but has sacrificed a superior breeding for C or D to breed B to Melvin.

And it does not end there. What does Lynnedora decide if, after breeding C, D comes into season before C is palpated? Does she gamble on two litters or four? We will leave her fate in the hands of the reader. In making your decision, remember that there is next year. If she breeds all four bitches, what does she do the following year? If she winds up with only two litters, where does she get bitch puppies for subsequent years?

Bitches

At the moment, our concern is the total population needed to establish an ongoing breeding program that can consistently produce three quality litters each year. As demonstrated above, you will need four quality two-year-old or older bitches and a large portion of luck to have a successful first year. (We will define a successful breeding year as one in which the breeder with a full-scale program produces three litters of pups, some of which pups equal or exceed the quality of their parents in terms of breed standards.)

"And what happens the following year? Do I have to buy four more two-year-old bitches to have a successful second year?"

Four more would provide a small comfort zone, but two and a large quantity of luck could get you through. Let's assume that all went perfectly well the first year. You bred A, C, and D to superior studs and kept a bitch puppy from each litter — Aa, Cc, and Dd. A, C, and D can be used again, with different studs, in the third year of operation. Aa, Cc, and Dd are your bitches for year five.

You will need to buy two more bitches, E and F, to team with B, the insurance bitch you did not breed the first year. If all goes well, you will breed B, E, and F the second year and again the fourth year. The bitch puppies you keep from the second year litters, Bb, Ee, and Ff, are your bitches for year six.

"That's a lot of bitches to provide for."

A lot, indeed. As you commence your third year, you will have a minimum of twelve bitches to feed and house. That makes for a considerable responsibility and no small work load. But remember, we're planning for maximums. If you are content with a two-litter year, or one litter, if you wish to forgo insurance bitches, the population can be reduced accordingly.

Always keep in mind, however, that numbers on paper do not always work in a breeding program. Even going to the maximums, there is no guarantee you can achieve consistency. One bitch in heat, for example, can draw others into heat. Well-spaced paper intervals can crumble into chaos when the breeder discovers there are six, eight, or ten bitches in heat at the same time.

Exercise and Run Facilities

Another thing. Do not relax with the thought that you can exercise all twelve bitches in one giant run together. Do all bitches get along? About as well as all people get along.

Two to a run can work; three pushes it; four strains and strains. We are not talking numbers of total animals, young and adult, male and female. We are saying that four bitches to a run, or in the house at the same time, for that matter, stretches a point. If one of those four is an alpha — a dominant — you may have three too many with her. We would estimate that you now need a minimum of four runs, sized accordingly for the breed.

For yard fencing, use the same chain link and gates that we discussed in yard fencing in *The Road to Westminster*. Each run will require its own gate, allowing a person entrance for cleaning. We suggest six-foot-high materials around the perimeter to keep large dogs and people out, as well as keeping your guys in. Since interior fencing is only to contain your dogs, size it accordingly. We use four-foot material internally.

Back to population. At any given time, along with your twelve bitches you may need room for a litter. Before they move out, there will be another litter. The litter area has to be away from the other animals. Depending on your breed, you could have from six to two dozen three- and four-month-olds running around. They need considerably more room than a whelping box offers.

Geriatrics

Also keep in mind your geriatrics. At this point, two of your bitches have already given you their two litters. They may be in line for retirement. If you intend to keep up your breeding stock, you must now make room for fourteen bitches, sixteen the year after, and so on until the first ones succumb.

Some breeders sell off their bitches as soon as their purpose is served. We would do that too, except for one glitch. Our bitches also become members of the family. For us, that's usually a lifetime commitment.

Do not misunderstand. Our position is only offered as one alternative. Many who plan a long-range program sell off the geriatrics. Their method is very much in keeping with modern business—use them up and ship them out.

In any event, your bitches will become geriatrics. If they remain, you may well want to consider special quarters to ease their advanced years. We'll come back to this topic in a bit.

Studs

Boys! All these bitches and no boys! If you are smart, you will keep it that way. Take the bitches out to stud or bring in cooled semen.

But, if you're like us, you won't be smart. You'll see a Best-in-Show winner among those beautiful boy puppies and have to keep just one. And if he falls somewhat short of expectations, just one more out of a subsequent litter. It is hard not to love those showy boys. Of course those cuddly girls grab your heart too.

Caution! Boys get along where there are no bitches. They even get along where there are bitches, until the hormones kick in or a bitch goes in heat. At that point the amiability of the boys toward each other soon ceases.

It shouldn't take much calculating to realize that you could wind up with a lot of animals in a hurry. And we have not counted them all yet. Add in the mistakes, the show dog that has his hips go bad, that blows a knee, or that ends up with a bad bite. Then, too, let's not forget the puppies. With a full-scale program, count on a population of twenty most days of the year.

LOGISTICS

Now that we know how many we are dealing with, give or take a half dozen, we need to discuss how we are going to deal with these numbers in terms of facility. Words fail us when we attempt to describe what the atmosphere in the kennel is like when three or four macho studs catch the scent of seven or eight bitches in heat. Your facility is very important at such times, for both animals and people. A stud dog becomes single-minded when there are bitches in heat, and he takes a dim view of anything, human or animal, friend or foe, that tries to interpose itself between stud and target.

How, then, do we arrange the runs? Each stud is assigned to a separate run, each with two or three bitches, none of which is in heat. We also make sure there is not more than one alpha bitch per run. This is the daytime arrangement. At night all sleep in their individual crates in the basement.

All bitches in heat are immediately separated from the general population and brought into the house. They eat in a house crate, sleep in a house crate, and exercise in a yard accessed through a doggy door from the kitchen. On those occasions that there is a male in the house, the bitches are confined to their crates and carefully watched.

Sounds easy enough, and it is. Well, it is sometimes. When four or five bitches come into heat at the same time that a litter is being delivered, it is not easy. Nor is it easy when the breeder daydreams and opens the wrong run gate at the wrong moment, allowing two males to gain access to the same area at the same time.

In all fairness to the boys, though, we hasten to add that our worst fights have occurred among dominant bitches. If you make a mistake with boys or girls and a brouhaha breaks out, do not try to step between. We can show scars that underline the folly of that strategy. The survival instinct takes over and the fighting bitches have no friends. If you try to grab a tail or the scruff of the neck, be careful. If you pull off only one, the other, sensing the advantage, may renew the attack. A garden hose and lots of cold water is your best bet. Always try to have a hose close by, making it easy for you to blast faces with cold water.

The next problem involves the arrangement of the runs. Runs are for exercise, not for living. The animals must be able to retreat to safe shelter during periods of inclement weather. They also need a place to sleep at night. This could be the same haven they retreat to when the weather threatens, or it could be a separate facility, a place where they will not likely disturb neighbors at two in the morning or be exposed to life-threatening weather. Measure each animal's crate to determine the minimum amount of overnight space you will require.

"Where do we find that much space?"

There are no easy answers, and as many answers as situations. We have seen people use closed-in and heated porches, extra first-floor rooms, basements, and converted garages. Several have built a separate kennel building at the end of the runs.

As you draw your plan to solve the problem, make certain you allow for easy transitions. We rely on doggy doors to give our animals access to both their daylight shelters and the overnight quarters where their crates await. Because we rely on doggy doors, we also curse a lot, especially when the doggy door fails to function or is eaten apart. The manufacturers of the doors must smile a lot. They charge almost as much for the replacement seals as for the original assembly. We do not smile much. We have seen new seals disappear within an hour or two of installation. Right after the better mousetrap, we need a better doggy door. We put men on the moon, didn't we?

One more thing with regard to the runs. Do not forget to install a people gate, one that affords easy, fast access. Cleaning, illnesses, fights, attempted surprise matings — be sure that you include that people gate.

"Does every breeder need runs?"

We think you can answer that for yourself. Twenty of any breed, even the smallest of the toys, would be several too many to run through the house every day.

If a breeder cannot afford extra buildings and does not have basements or garages, he should wait until he can afford something of the kind. Keep in mind that we are describing the deluxe package. We said at the beginning that breeders should only attempt what they can do well.

"But buildings take time. Is there an interim possibility, something temporary until buildings can be finished, or basements readied for multiple occupancy?"

Reluctantly we offer an alternative, but only for the interim until buildings can be finished or basements readied for multiple occupancy. You can equip each run with a doghouse for each animal in the run. We discussed criteria for such structures in *The Road to Westminster*, but we will give an overview here. Insulate where the climate demands, protect animals against drafts, and plan a removable roof for easy cleaning. If the breeders live in an area that gets real, dangerous winter, they may well consider one large doghouse with room for four, rather than individual structures. The advantage to the animals is that they can then cuddle and share body heat, much as a litter does.

To avoid any misunderstanding, we do not condone keeping an animal outside around the clock. (We acknowledge that there are some few breeds that are bred to be outside and prefer remaining outside.) We strenuously object on behalf of the poor creatures who are tied out without water, adequate housing, or love. At our kennel, there is a hard and fast rule that no puppy will ever leave with someone who intends to keep it outside. The rule is incorporated into our sales contract.

FEEDING

For breeders with a full complement of animals, feeding becomes a real treat. There can be twenty stainless steel bowls to juggle — some filled with low protein food for geriatrics, others with high protein rations for animals on the show circuit or in the field. Most of the animals get regular protein in the 22% range. Oh, yes, lest we forget, there are special mixes for pregnant and postnatal moms. And the puppies too!

Gone are the days of stopping by the supermarket and buying a bag of some popular brand, or buying an alleged super-mix from the vet at ten dollars more per bag. We discussed food in *The Road to Westminster*. Stick with what you selected after reading that information, if you can. Just adjust the protein levels to the various needs. Remember, too much protein is not better.

What you will now need to do is find a distributor who can bring you five hundred pounds at a time, at a volume price. In our part of the country you would expect an invoice total between two and three hundred dollars for that quantity. Those first few invoices grab your attention. Sometimes you can find other breeders or dog owners in the area who use the same product, and you can join forces to gain a better price.

We will warn you ahead of time that the food companies are about as cooperative as a tornado. Many times you have to beg them for the name of a distributor, then beg again for a delivery of less than two thousand pounds. We have now made three major brand changes because of lack of availability. Someone needs to have a long talk with those executives who make the big bucks and do not do the job.

"I'm also going to need room to store all that food."

Indeed you are. You will need a space cool and dry and mouseless. We empty our food from the bags into plastic garbage cans—the heavy duty, thirty-two gallon size. No mice, no mold.

Try to arrange your storage area near your crates. That many dishes makes for a lot of trips. Add in the moms and pups you have in a separate area, and your legs and arms will soon weary.

By the same token, do not allow dawdling. Make one trip to the crate with the food; another trip, fifteen minutes later, for the empty bowl. Not empty! Too bad! Away it goes. It will be empty tomorrow.

Water

You will need more water pails, at least one per run, hooked to the fence with one of those double-ended clips. In winter, those who live in the north will have to keep the water in the warm shelter areas so that the water does not freeze. The closer the source of water is to the destination of the water, the better it will be for the breeder and the breeder's back. A suggestion to save time: wash your feed dishes while you are at the water supply filling your buckets.

EXERCISE

Runs help satisfy the animal's need for exercise, allowing the animal to exercise himself. But that will not do the whole job for the medium- and large-size breeds. To muscle up, at least the medium- and large-size kids need the challenge of uphill and downhill along with a variety of surfaces.

There is one valuable assistant available to the breeder when exercising the troops. It is a flexible lead that uncoils from a spool to a length of twenty-five feet, then retracts at the push of a button. What a wonderful invention! Puppy travels out and back, out and back, while breeder strolls leisurely. With twenty to exercise, every saved step is important.

The animals need one mile a day, too. Sounds like a problem, doesn't it? Not enough hours in the day? Well, you could try two animals at a time. That will cut the task to ten trips per day, five hours more or less. That does not include the time to unwrap the leads from trees and other such obstacles when the two animals decide to take off in separate directions.

But not many of even the most dedicated breeders have that kind of time to devote to exercising our animals on a daily basis. The breeder can only do the best he can. The animals can go farther, faster than we can. Some people use a bicycle to exercise the dogs, others a motor vehicle. Under the right conditions that should not be dangerous. Try a country lane, with one person driving and the handler on the tailgate of a wagon or pickup. Match the vehicle's speed to the animal's gait. Do not make the animal match the vehicle.

Still you may not get to everyone, especially during bad weather. The thing to do is to keep a chart. That way everyone gets an equal share of whatever you can give. Make each outing a quality outing. Snow and sand build muscle. Hills do too. Vary surfaces you exercise on — stone, grass, and concrete.

FOUL WEATHER

Foul weather is a nightmare for most breeders. Those of us who live in the north know that cold makes everything more difficult. Walks get slippery, latches and clips will not open, gates refuse to swing. It is not much fun. Plan for it.

Warm climate people have to worry about shade and water supply. Conditions there favor worms, fleas, and contagions. Both people and animals need to show caution when exercising in the heat. Especially dangerous are hot concrete and macadam. Your animal does not wear shoes.

For very many breeders, no matter where they live, rain and mud make the worst enemies. Hosing off a couple dozen dogs, spreading towels in crates for them to dry on, washing the towels — these are the joys of rainy weather. After two weeks of rain or a long January thaw, you will have all you want of rain and mud.

Concrete versus Stone

"What if we go to the expense of installing concrete runs?"

Concrete runs certainly make it easier to keep the animals clean. They are great for places like boarding kennels, where animals only spend a few days at a time. We do not recommend it for breeding kennels; not day in and day out. Think about what concrete does to the legs and backs of people who have to work on it all the time.

Dogs certainly never encountered concrete in the wild. Their owners worry about what their charges ate before domestication, duplicating those nutrients in the food they feed, but they show no concern when those same animals pound back and forth over concrete every day of their lives.

The best thing we have found is stone — two inches of 2B stone topped with six inches of river washed pea rock. (2B is a term used by lumber yards for rock size.) Yes, the stone will settle and have to be topped off now and again. Yes, the animals can and will dig huge holes. Yes, dogs on stone will still get dirty. Certainly they will be a lot less dirty than those on grass or the ground, but they won't stay as clean as on concrete.

The worst part of stone is the installation. If you install your fencing first, make sure your design allows a tractor access. We can promise you that spreading a couple hundred tons of stone with a wheelbarrow, rake, and shovel is not fun at all. Obviously there are also positives, or we would not use it. Stone does not get as cold or hot as concrete. Urine drains, rather than making puddles for the animals to run through and roll on. Stones do not crack when settling or break up when heaved by frost.

Most important of all, stone is good for the animals. The poundings suffered on concrete are eliminated. Stone offers a much cleaner environment than ground. It also presents a shifting surface that requires the animals to utilize their muscles to counteract it. They build their muscle mass on their outings and keep it toned on the stone.

POOPER-SCOOPING

This task certainly takes on a new dimension. You now have twenty animals making daily deposits. That makes for a lot of poop.

In hot weather you may want to scoop two or three times a day to improve odor and fly control. If those little missed dribs and drabs mount up and flies become a problem, pick a sunny day and crate the animals for a couple of hours. Attach a bottle-sprayer to your hose, set it at 16:1 or 12:1, fill the bottle with chlorine bleach, and spray every inch of the runs thoroughly.

After two hours in a good sun, it should be safe to run out the animals again. As an added precaution, we usually give the area a good flush with clear water first, then run out the dogs. In the meantime, the flies disappear and the area smells fresher.

In the winter, you have less time to accomplish your scoopings before darkness becomes a problem. Those who work a full day find this a severe problem. Many leave for work in darkness and return home in darkness. When does the scooping get done?

We wish there was a clever response to offer. One possibility is to assign that task to the children. You will not make them happy, but they are usually home from school before dark. Those without children can perhaps rent one of the neighbors' children.

Short of that alternative, we suggest a large flashlight. Do not make the mistake of thinking that you can let the snow cover and break down the feces before spring. It does not happen. Come the thaw, your animals will be hock deep in a swamp of feces. While you valiantly hose and rake and whatever else, the dogs track it inside, walk on rugs and furniture, and wipe their feet on your clothes. They stink, the house stinks, you stink, the facility stinks. It only takes a day or two for a proud facility to become a tragedy.

To make things worse, as if they could get worse, it usually works out that the day you have dogs that need bathing and a poop-covered facility, is exactly the day that your food shipment will arrive. As the truck pulls away and you are sweat covered from unloading, expect the arrival of those people who are interested in a puppy or the family trying to decide if your breed is right for them.

"White dogs are especially wonderful to have at times like that."

No doubt about it. White dog breeders are the martyrs of the sport. We should all live in places like Arizona.

Now comes the problem of what to do with it. That is no small problem and there is no easy answer. Those with large property holdings can dig holes and layer them with lime. Most of us have to collect it in plastic bags and send it off with the garbage. (You need to be careful with this though. Some areas now have laws against animal feces being in garbage picked up by the city or count.)

Sounds easy, but it becomes an art form at times. Because we have limits on how much garbage we can put out each week, we collect in white bags and combine those in larger, heavyweight trash bags. If you use a rake and avoid picking up a lot of stone, everything goes pretty smoothly in dry weather.

In wet weather, seven bags of poop from twenty animals can weigh a good bit. Carefully mix the poop bags with the house garbage to produce an end result that the poor garbageman can lift to the truck. If the bag is too heavy and the man leaves it there, you really have a problem the following week.

EXPENSES

We discussed facilities earlier. The expense of the additional fencing, gates, and stone necessary to handle twenty dogs, as compared to one, is a hefty expense. We are talking numbers in the thousands here. Be careful! Do not exhaust all your cash resources on facilities and have nothing left for day-to-day operations.

New animals added to the breeding stock will also cost money. As we will discuss later, you want quality additions. Stocking yourself with mediocre bitches will not get you off to a strong start. If your goal is to improve the breed, start with the best specimens available to date and pay the price.

An increased food bill follows in the wake of an increased population. Smaller items such as collars, leads, etc., will add up too. Of course you can use the same collar and lead on more than one dog, but you want some flexibility.

"Do I have to get licenses for every animal?"

One way or another. In our state, it is possible to purchase one kennel license that covers all the dogs. In addition to the expense of twenty-five to thirty dollars here, there is also an inspection by a dog officer. If you fear such an inspection, you should probably move on to wind surfing as your sport and forget breeding. The dog law officer wants you to succeed.

Closely related are the required shots and vaccinations. Meet the veterinarian. More animals, more shots, more illnesses, more injuries, more vet bills. The sequence, especially for a novice, is inescapable.

"Why 'especially for a novice'?"

The veterans learn that they can purchase the same serums as the vets and can give their own shots. Likewise, they learn to recognize maladies that recur and to apply the proper remedies.

The wise breeder learns to strike a happy medium. A breeder is not in business to build a new wing on the animal hospital. Neither does he challenge the vet's expertise with the complex problems and surgeries. The breeder knows he cannot survive without the vet. Many vets, however, make a good living from the society trade, and would rather not face the challenges posed by breeders who know their animals.

In *The Road to Westminster*, we discussed the choice of a vet. The potential breeder would do well to review that section and be assured he has made the right choice.

Please keep in mind that, at this point, we are only discussing expenses connected with increasing the population. To be sure, multiple show entries will dent the bank balance. You will also have to face the prospect of a new vehicle, one that can transport multiple entries.

GROOMING

There is another area we have not yet touched. With multiple animals to be maintained and potentially multiple show entrants to be groomed, the old grooming table, folded and stored in a closet, will no longer meet your need. While you're finding space for everything else, the breeder bent on a full-scale program must make room for a permanent grooming area and fill it with all the proper supplies.

A permanent area is easy to use. You walk in with the animal and start work, with everything you need in easy reach. If the area is under-supplied or difficult to use, however, routine tasks become problems, and problems become crises. Worse, hit and miss grooming replaces dependable routines. What you need is an area with excellent lighting, brightly colored walls, and an easy-to-maintain floor covering. Also check the number of outlets and circuits available in the area for dryers, clipper vacs, and such.

(Again we want to avoid breed-specific recommendations. The breeder you purchase from is without question the best source of information for specific items necessary to the grooming of your particular breed.)

After lighting, the problem of bathing should claim your attention. There is no joy in bending over a floor tub or lifting heavy animals into a waist-high tub. As the years pass, there is even less joy. Whether stainless steel or porcelain, mount the tub at a height that is convenient for you.

The next problem is getting the animal up to the height that is convenient for you. Unless you have little guys, do not risk your back bending and lifting. If you have room, build a ramp that allows the animal to walk up to the tub. If that proves impractical, buy the hydraulic table you have been planning to buy and use it to elevate the animal. Then simply lift him across to the tub, or use a portable catwalk.

Make sure you equip the tub with a non-skid surface and a hose for rinsing. A restraint noose is not a bad idea either. Converting the area under the tub into a storage area for towels, shampoos, and such is ideal. Always keep those materials within easy reach so that you never have to abandon the animal while bathing it.

You don't need to retire your faithful folding table. It still travels. But at home you need something sturdy that will lower to animal size, then elevate Throck to the right height for you.

Though it may sound expensive, it is less expensive than a slipped disc. There are several kinds and sizes of such tables, electric and foot pump models. What you need is a table with a base that will not tip; a non-skid work surface adequate in size for your breed; a smoothly operating lift; an easily adjusted, stable grooming arm.

Unless you intend to become a professional groomer one day, or you plan to add a second breed, you do not need all the accessories that equip the table to handle Danes to Papillons. Nor do you need those expensive touches that may well make life easier for the person who grooms all day, every day, but will get little use by the breeder.

Your table should be in the most well-lighted part of the room. The light should come from above and behind you as you work. A mirror on the wall, opposite the way you face when you work, will make it easy to check the animal's profile.

If the grooming area is near where you keep the crates, so much the better. If not, you may want to make room for one or two crates to hold animals you're in the process of bathing.

You will also need a rack or pegboard, located within easy reach of the table. That's where you keep the combs, clippers, etc. If the table comes with drawers or cabinets, better yet.

On the subject of hand-held equipment, as we mentioned earlier, we would rather defer to those working with the reader's particular breed. We can, however, furnish you with a list of grooming tools to ask about. Those of you who read *The Road to Westminster* probably have many of the following, as well as a tack box to put them in:

Brushes	Nail trimmers
Clippers and blades	Scissors
Combs	Shears
Mat splitters	Thinning shears

You will also want to ask about supplies such as shampoos and conditioners.

In total, we are talking a good sum of money. Keep in mind, though, that we are describing a full-scale program. Most of us start small and work toward these goals as money and superior animals become available. You should be aware, however, that no matter where you start, the financial drain is large and constant.

OBLIGATIONS

In addition to the financial drain, you must also think of your obligations to animals, family, and neighbors.

Your obligation to the animals extends through all seven days of each week, all fifty-two weeks of each year, and all ten to fifteen years of that animal's life. That's a lot of obligation for anyone. Food, water, health care, grooming, shelter, exercise, lots and lots of love — you will have to supply all of these.

There is also the obligation to the family. You started out going to shows as a team. Now you're creating a situation where someone will have to stay home with the troops if the show is any distance away. Animals do not stop eating because you want to enjoy a weekend any more readily than they sleep late on holidays and weekends.

Both problems can be solved by recruiting a trustworthy person who loves animals, who will agree to training, and whom you pay to kennel-sit. Do it! You will still be able to enjoy the sport as a family. The reward is well worth the time to recruit and train.

Do not forget the neighbors. More animals can mean more voices. A dog that might seldom bark under house conditions can often be induced to join the crowd by his peers. The fire whistle will coax a howling from our Clumbers and Shepherds every time.

Fair is fair. Your neighbor cannot expect that your animals will never bark, just as you cannot expect that his mower will never shatter your serenity. At the same time, you should not expect the neighbors to lose sleep night after night. We solve the problem by crating our animals from 10 p.m. to 6 a.m. Though Clumbers are not given to barking a lot, they will respond to the dogs of less considerate neighbors who tie their animals to a tree and let them bay at the moon.

Without exception, the most difficult obligation for us to fulfill is the equal giving and receiving of love. When we only had Christina, we took her everywhere, bought her milkshakes, and played fetch and cuddle. We made her life happy and she did the same for us. You cannot take twenty dogs for a ride, just as you cannot hold twenty on your lap. If you take none for fear of hurting the others, everyone loses.

We try. Our intention is to rotate all of the animals into the house at some time during the day for some personal attention. Rides are assigned by turns. Does it work? No! At least not often. A hundred things surface to shatter the schedules — weather, heat cycles, puppies, time shortage. Still we try.

EMOTIONAL IMPACT

How does one describe the pain of watching a bitch die while giving birth? The poor bitch gets put with a male she may or may not know, is commanded to stand and receive him, then agonizes through a pregnancy that causes her death.

Yes, the pups then have to be raised by humans and bottle-fed. That is the least of the problem. The most of the problem is carrying that poor mother to the cemetery and burying her. The most of the problem is trying to explain to her and yourself why it happened that way.

Fortunately, the odds overwhelmingly favor the bitch performing well. She probably will not be the focus of your sadness. More than likely the mummy puppy, or the water puppy, or the stillborn will cause the tears. They happen and there is nothing much we can do about it. Even worse is when a full-term puppy spends too much time in the birth canal and suffocates.

And some of the born will not make it. Even though they're delivered, dried, weighed, and squirming with the rest, crib deaths, low sugar, brain damage, and more can send you to the cemetery again and again through the years. There will be many times that you think you cannot stand one more death, one more trip to the vet to put another animal down. Some breeders take them to the vet with the first hint of a problem, before they get attached. Others believe in giving love until the babies start hurting. Neither choice is easy and both end in tears.

Selling the puppies is far from a picnic either. You are not burying them, but in many cases you are sending them out of your life forever. The consolation, so they tell us, is in knowing the puppy will live a happy life with his new people, loving and being loved. And that is true, but it still hurts.

Finally comes the day when the old friends start to falter. A decade and some, not much more, and that only with luck. This is the worst time of all and is like burying your children.

REWARDS

Breeding also provides many, many, many happinesses. Not the least of them is the family togetherness that you are already enjoying. Any time you can come up with a project that the whole family enjoys, you have a winner. All too soon the human children go off to new homes too.

You will see a lot of people at the shows without their families. That can work too. One adult enjoys showing dogs, the children are at a peer party, the other adult shoots a round of golf. Breathing room for the family offers its merits too. Breeding, however, is a good deal more demanding than showing. If the family refuses to help and derides your efforts, the situation could soon turn ugly.

Life, not death, is what breeding should be about. We have no words to describe the joy of a healthy litter and the knowledge that you played some little part in bringing them into the world.

Wait until the first time a litter spots you coming home and charges across the yard to love you. Eyes sparkling, little legs churning, tails on permanent wag — their single objective is to love their person. Suddenly all of the time, expense, and pain melt away and you know why you are a breeder.

Do not resist loving that litter and being loved. Some breeders do, calculating that puppy sales will then be objective. Even if that is true and it hurts less, think of all the missed love.

What is more, the loved and often-handled puppy will make a quick adjustment when it goes to a family where the puppy will be the center of attention. Certainly the new parents will be better off for the addition. When the new parents start arriving for their puppies and tears blur the breeders' vision, the breeders need to think of the times they wanted to take all of their adults for ice cream and could not possibly do it. The breeder cannot keep them all.

Somewhere down the road, if you are very lucky and hold up through it all, the final reward will come. One of your animals will stand Best-in-Show at Westminster. And the best part will be overhearing a knowledgeable dog person say he can spot dogs from your kennel any time. Coats, rears, heads, fronts—whatever he underlines, you will know your efforts have impacted the breed. We wish you all wisdom and that your impact may bring a true improvement to your breed.

3.

The Breeding Program

One more time we would like to underline the point that Chapter 2 describes a maximum breeding program. It is for those with deep assets and an absolute mind fix.

A CONSERVATIVE BREEDING PROGRAM _____

Most of us have shallower assets and some doubts as to the extent to which we are prepared to carry our commitment when we start breeding animals. We use the maximum program as a master plan to which we aspire and accomplish one small step at a time. Take stock after living with each addition. If family and animals are still smiling, reach out again.

We cannot remember ever urging anyone to maximize immediately. In Lynnedora's case, we suggested she find a suitable stud for Throckmortana and go from there. Although we have talked about the joy and pain of breeding, no one in Lynnedora's family knows for certain how he will respond to the actuality. And they certainly do not have a lot of extra money to spend on a facility they will never use. Take one small step at a time.

GENETICS _____

"Where do we start looking and what are we looking for?"

This is the point where breeders usually run to their library and treat the novice to stacks of books offering long and detailed explanations on the workings of genetics, from Mendel to the most recent isolations. Read one or more of those books. If nothing else, you will learn that only the most outrageous luck could bring about any significant and lasting changes to the breed in anything that resembles a short period of time.

There is a glitch! Most people only read the first few pages of those books. The paragraphs of those pages tell them that if you put a black cocker and a buff cocker together, out of four pups you should get one black, two mixed, and one buff. They never say what happens if there are six pups, or seven.

That's enough, they tell themselves. They close the book and start breeding. A quarter of everything they produce, so they think, will be wonderful. Use a Champion stud and a Champion bitch, that is the ticket. A quarter of the litter will be Best-in-Show material. What could be easier than that?

Not much could be easier, if it really worked that way. Unfortunately, many breeders, some of whom have been breeding for years, will still advise those who come to them that that is the way it works. Worse, even though they see evidence in their litters to the contrary, they themselves still believe what they disseminate. It was in a book, chart and all. It must be true.

They should have turned the page. It is certainly true that out of every ten thousand puppies issuing from a black-buff parentage, the ratio should turn out to be 3:1. But that does not mean that each litter will produce at 3:1. The only reason we can hazard a guess on ten thousand is that color is controlled by a single gene.

After color, however, we run into more complex problems and the predictions stop. When we talk about components such as head size, straight front, and rear drive, we are isolating structures that involve tens, hundreds, or thousands of genes. A particular head shape could involve dominant genes, partially expressed dominants, or recessives. Think of the possible combinations we are building and you will begin to understand the complexities.

Inbreeding

As in most facets of life, there are those who will come up with the simple fix. Inbreed! Father to daughter, mother to son, brother to sister. That will help fix the strengths. Of course it will also emphasize the weaknesses. Who does the burying if it turns out that the weaknesses dominate the strengths?

Now do not misunderstand. We are certainly not condemning inbreeding. It will bring out the facets of a line more quickly. That a lot of substandard puppies may have to be destroyed can be defended by those who inbreed under the old "end justifying the means" premise. Perhaps it does justify the means. It is a question for each breeder to decide and live with.

Line Breeding

For those who would like to cut down the odds of the crap shoot, but are unwilling to risk the gamble of inbreeding, we offer line breeding. Line breeding is a modified inbreeding. Aunt to nephew, uncle to niece, grandchildren to grandparents, etc. The inbreeders tell us it is the system used by those who fear the word incest. Whether that is true or not, loose line breeding or tight line, it is certainly the most popular method.

Outcrossing

The other possibility is outcrossing, or breeding to some non-related or distantly related animal. Most assuredly that will increase the uncertainty involved. It is done in the hope of bringing vigor back to the line, or of introducing a characteristic from the new line that is not previously apparent in the old line.

We can explain with an example. Throck is a very feminine looking bitch. We prefer that clear distinction between the look of a bitch and the look of a male. Some do not. Especially in this era of unisex, there are those who prefer softer looking males and doggy bitches. (Doggy bitches are those that lack the feminine look and more closely resemble the dogs of the breed than the bitches.) Since the line they are working with lacks doggy bitches, they may seek out a bitch that looks very masculine and breed to her.

The odds do not favor them if they only go that far. Why would they believe that that bitch can pass on her characteristic? And if she can, how does the breeder know the stud will not dominate the breeding and negate the bitch's contributions? It is a real crap shoot.

"So what is best for us and Throck? Should we just pick one of the big winning males and roll the dice, or should I go to a college and enroll in a genetics course?"

More education never hurt anyone, but college should not be necessary and a genetics course at that level could lead you off into avenues you really have no interest in pursuing. Let's try another way.

OBSERVE THE BREED

It was no accident that Throck won her championship easily. Lynnedora searched out judges who knew a bad Clumber from a good Clumber and took them an animal of merit. Throck, therefore, can be considered her foundation bitch, the keystone around which Lynnedora will build.

First step, objectively compare the A.K.C. recognized breed standard for Clumbers to real Clumbers, past and present. What head pleases you and is in keeping with the standard? What body type? Travel to Clumber kennels if you can. Take pictures. Look at yearbooks and other Club publications that might provide photos of departed friends. Your objective is to put together a composite of what you see as the perfect Clumber male and the perfect Clumber female, always with the limits imposed by the standard.

Do not be afraid to discuss your mission with established breeders. Listen to their interpretations of the standard and their descriptions of the perfect Clumber.

At every opportunity—during your visits to the other kennels, at shows—watch the breed in motion. Watch home movies or television tapes. Movement, movement, movement. Develop the best eye you can for proper breed movement and what structures produce it.

Now let's go back to our friend Throck. Take your composite type Clumber and your composite moving Clumber and divide them into parts, including every aspect mentioned in the standard. Your list may start with head, eyes, nose, and so on. Assign each feature a point value, then score Throck.

Head just what you want — ten. Nose the right color — ten. Muzzle a trifle too long—eight and a half. Proceed through the whole standard. It will take some time and concentration, but will be well worth the effort.

Once you finish, you will have a more precise idea of those of Throck's qualities you would like to carry forward through your breeding efforts. You will also be able to focus on the areas you would like to upgrade or change radically.

CHOOSE A DIRECTION

You cannot do it all at once, and do not focus only on the area of cosmetics. If you often found structural faults during your search, perhaps your primary objective will be to breed one of those problems out of your lines.

Whatever direction you pick, focus on it. Do one thing at a time. Do not become so preoccupied that you let other qualities deteriorate. But by the same token, do not dilute your capacities by trying to do it all.

For our example, we shall go with muzzle length because it is easier to talk about and more certainly genetic than some of the more severe health and structural problems.

Let's assume you believe Throck's muzzle is a tad long, making her look just the least bit houndy. You have researched and consulted. You are certain that shortening the muzzle that same tad will improve appearance without penalizing breathing and stamina in the field. (A Clumber should be able to hunt all day.)

The first thing we want to do is rate the muzzles on parents and grandparents. Lynnedora is in luck because we have both parents and all grandparents in residence. If your breeder does not, ask for pictures, or, at least, the best recollections.

In Throck's case, the muzzles in neither her mother's nor her father's lines are consistent, suggesting we have no fixed set of dominant genes operating in this line to determine muzzle length. That's the good news.

The bad news is that there could be several thousand genes that produce the muzzle. In those thousands, how many are culprits? How many cause the longer muzzle? The culprits could be as few as one. That's correct — to produce consistent muzzle lengths, it may be necessary to isolate one gene in thousands and change it. The odds against that happening are worse than the odds against winning the lottery. Much worse!

The best the breeder can do is pick a stud from one of the other lines in the breed that has a muzzle of the desired length. More ideally, the stud's father and grandfather will also display muzzles of the desired length. It is not a certainty, but at least three generations in a row allow for some optimism that shorter muzzles are dominant in the stud's line and could pass to his progeny.

Then again, that short muzzle could result from a collection of persistent recessive genes, which could be dominated by the gene or genes in the bitch that produce longer muzzles. The breeder could, therefore, be blessed with a litter in which every muzzle matches his ideal. Unfortunately, the breeder could also be blessed with a litter in which only some or none of the puppies grow to have the desired muzzle.

Let's try another scenario. Though we cannot find a stud with the desired muzzle, we do want to breed Throck. Let's let our imagination run wild and suppose we find that there are as many as half a dozen quality stud dogs available. How do we choose the proper sire for our first litter?

We take out some lined paper and make a list of Throck's strengths and weaknesses. The next step is to call the owners of the studs and ask them each for a similar list. (If you are starting your program with a stud and you are looking for a bitch, use the same method.) Once you receive the lists, play the matching game. The stud that shows the most strengths in areas where Throck has weaknesses is the likely choice.

At this point, the breeder has his paper tigers. The only problem is that paper tigers do not always work, much like a football team that on paper cannot lose, yet never wins a game.

THE BITCH

In this example, the foundation bitch is Throckmortana, and we know her well. At least we think we do. Say she is a little past two years old and a maiden. Any younger would make us wonder if she had the physical and mental maturity to mother a litter and care for it.

Keep track of the length of intervals between a bitch's heat cycles. If you know approximately when she is due, you can watch for the early signs and better count the days to ovulation. It is discouraging to find your bitch in full-blown heat and have to guess when she started, especially if you intend to take her out for stud service.

If ever there was a time for exercise, this is it. You want the bitch to be in the very best muscle tone she can be for the ordeal ahead. For at least a month before her cycle (another reason to keep records) get her out every day for the full regimen — at least a mile of uphill, downhill, and various surfaces. Snow builds muscle, as do sand and water. Continue to exercise her after she comes in season, but be careful where. A bitch in heat may attract more trouble than you are prepared to deal with.

To date, no hereditary or congenital defects have shown up in Throck. But a routine physical by the vet during that preceding month may well pay dividends. You should request a blood test for brucellosis and a stool analysis for parasites. At the start of the cycle, we routinely put our bitches on tetracycline until the first breeding. The medication will clear up any low grade vaginal infections. It can also cause dark teeth in puppies. Stop the medication with the first breeding.

THE STUD

In our model situation, Lynnedora would not own the stud. After careful research, she would select the boy who, on paper, looks to have the most to offer Throck's babies. We can even imagine that our choice has been used at stud before. This gives us a chance to have a look at some of his offspring to see where he appears to dominate.

Confirmed in our estimates he can potentially contribute, with no negative evidence, we conclude Pedunk is the best stud we can find. We next have to contact his owner and furnish her with a pedigree and pictures. If she wants to meet us somewhere, at a show site, for instance, to have a hands-on meeting with the bitch, we can arrange that also.

Of course we are still imagining our model. In reality, the stud may well live two or three thousand miles away. That only complicates the situation. The bitch owner must still convince the owner of the Champion stud that the bitch is a worthy mate and why.

We know that both mother and father will contribute equally to the progeny, but an amazing number of people, experienced and not, still believe the stud dominates every breeding. If the puppies turn out poorly, they are quick to blame the stud.

Little wonder that the stud owner exercises caution. The more she has spent finishing his championship and campaigning him as a special, the more cautious she will tend to be. More cautious still if it's his first time. A great litter can assure his career as a stud. A mediocre to poor litter can end that career.

BREEDING PAPERWORK

To allow our model breeding to progress, we shall assume that Pedunk lives in Oregon. Lynnedora talks to his owner at length, mails her the pedigree and pictures, and receives a return call to say the stud owner agrees to the match. Ecstasy! Our little bitch is going to be a mother and we are going to be breeders.

As soon as the euphoria passes, the realization sets in that there are still some matters to be resolved, not the least of which is the stud service contract. Remember, as you study the wording, that one day you may well be issuing stud service contracts if you continue breeding. Walk in the shoes of both stud and bitch owner before you accept or reject provisions.

Without getting into specific wording, the stud owner should certainly be expected to protect both her animal and his reputation. To that end, she has every right to request a health certificate certifying the kinds and dates of shots. Some also want to see the results of a brucellosis test.

In return, the stud owner should also provide a health certificate and assurance the stud is free of brucellosis. Your bitch is just as valuable to you as her stud is to her. In addition, the stud owner should be willing to have a sperm count done, in conjunction with a motility and morphology assessment. What you should expect is a sperm count in excess of 250 million per ejaculate. We like to see a progressive motility of 80%, more or less. That simply means that 80% of the sperm swim in a straight line. Abnormal morphology includes sperm without heads, or coiled and kinked tails. The bitch owner will then be assured that the stud will deliver a more than sufficient number of active sperm to do the job.

The choice of where the breeding will take place belongs to the stud owner. Traditionally, the bitch travels to the stud. That is not, however, written in stone. Sometimes both travel, meeting at a mutual friend's or a midway motel. On occasion, if the stud owner is a novice and the bitch owner an experienced breeder, the stud owner seizes the opportunity to learn and travels to the bitch owner. Wherever it takes place, the stud owner should promise a certificate of mating, confirming that the breeding took place and whether it was natural or an artificial insemination.

Be assured that there will be a section of the contract devoted to expected remuneration. What does the stud owner expect in return for her time and her stud's services? Sit down for this one.

Only kidding. Most stud owners are very fair. They will charge approximately the price of a show grade puppy for a successful attempt, or a puppy of their choice. We reject any provision that guarantees a puppy. We prefer to pay the fee in cash and consider all the puppies ours. Should the stud owner then wish to buy a puppy from the litter, she will certainly be treated as a preferred customer.

If the stud owner has spent a lot of money campaigning the stud around the country, advertising, and piling up Group and Best-in-Show wins, expect the price to double or more. Only the stud owner can know how much she has invested and how much she must recoup to continue her program. Some get carried away, expecting the bitch owners to pay for exorbitant expenditures. Do not do it. If she wants more than Pedunk is worth to your program, go to the next stud on the list. Your program requires money to continue also.

There are also times when a novice gets lucky and buys a super stud the first time around. Often the novice is so excited, especially if the bitch owner is a name in the breed, that he will agree to anything, even letting you use the stud for free. Do not do that! Arrange for some form of payment. Later on, when the stud owner is experienced, there will be no feeling that you took advantage of his inexperience.

You may also find a clause that states a certain charge will be assessed for time and trouble whether the breeding takes or not. If the breeding is successful, it is deducted from stud fees. These charges are usually minimal and well earned.

We are happy to say that among several of the Clumber owners, there is still enough trust to make contracts unnecessary. In other breeds it is the same. When you reach the point where you are taken at your word and a phone call covers it all, you will know you have paid your dues.

TRAVELING TO BREED

"We mailed the contract back. The stud's owner said they want Throck a week early and that we should call with flight information."

Now you have to get your bitch to the stud, which may involve distances requiring airline travel. The idea of this makes breeders very nervous and brings up legitimate concerns. Your animal will travel as luggage. We make jokes about our suitcases being lost or damaged, but there is no humor when the lost or damaged luggage is your animal.

Does it happen? Yes. Have animals died? Yes. But there are things you can do to improve her chances and almost guarantee Throck's safety. Is there a positive side? A best guess says that less than one-tenth of one percent of the million animals flown every year suffers negative incidents.

To avoid your dog being one of those few, start by purchasing a proper fiberglass airline kennel for her. All airports sell them and many pet shops do. Without getting into brand names, we prefer the type that are fattest in the center, receding at top and bottom. Put two together and you will notice that the central bulge prevents the crates from being stacked so tightly that the air vents are blocked. Pad the bottom with something that won't hurt the animal if she eats it. Cedar shavings or newspaper works.

Book her on a through flight if at all possible. The more plane changes there are, the more opportunity for mistakes. Among her worst enemies are heat and cold. Some airlines offer a special handling service that assures she will be special delivered to the plane and loaded immediately. At the other end she will be taken off first and specialled to the terminal.

If you can find such a service, the peace of mind is well worth the slight extra cost. To further stack the odds for Throck, book an early morning or late evening flight, when tarmacs and loading docks are cool. If the service breaks down and she sits under the cargo hold, at least she will not be in the sun. Do not forget to pay for her open return.

Stop feeding Throck at least six to twelve hours before she flies. You do not want to risk the dog choking or fouling in flight. Throck will not require tranquilizers; most dogs do not.

Get to the airport early and exercise her before you turn her over. Make sure the crate is clearly marked with easily read letters. Use such things as the following: Live Animals! Avoid Cold! Avoid Heat! Keep Level! Also make certain that your name, address, and phone number cannot be missed. Place your valid health certificate in the appropriate envelope.

If the airport will allow you to accompany the animal to the loading zone, do it. Talk to the people who will load her. At most airports you can find a window or observation deck that will allow you to watch the actual loading. Even at a distance, you will be able to spot a crate. If there are several, assume yours is one.

When you see the crate go on, smile. But do not get complacent. Once the cargo door closes, there is no oxygen or cooling in that compartment until the plane is underway. That should only be a short interval. If takeoff is for some reason inordinately delayed, contact a representative and insist the airline open the cargo door.

Assuming the person at the other end has all the pertinent information — flight number, weigh bill number, E.T.A. — there is nothing more you can do. Once the plane starts down the runway, you can only suffer until that call comes from Pedunk's mom, assuring you Throck is safely arrived.

We ourselves seldom fly animals and never fly them for breeding. We will drive them twelve hours one way, but no flying. Before you get more nervous than you are, we should say that our refusal to fly animals for breeding has little to do with our lack of confidence in the airlines. Actually, we have never had anything but good experiences when we did fly animals to clients or shows.

In fact, there was a time when we did fly bitches for breeding. Not one of them ever came back pregnant. Now that could have been pure coincidence. More than likely it was. But after three or four, we decided to reevaluate.

Our conclusion was that flying a bitch, who would then live with strangers and be mauled by a strange stud, imposed one degree of stress too many. They experienced no difficulties when we drove them. It was the same bitch to the same stud and this time puppies resulted. We make no pretense that two or three similar instances constitute unimpeachable evidence. Bitches do fly and conceive. All except ours, that is.

"Is there a reasonable compromise? We cannot drive all the way to Oregon, but we certainly do not want to stress Throck."

Call Pedunk's owner. She wants Throck a week ahead of time to allow her to adjust. Tell the breeder that you will fly with Throck and bring her in a day or two before she is ready. Though that won't help Throck during the flight, there will be a friend greeting her when she comes off the plane.

Ask Pedunk's mother for the number of the motel nearest her home and announce your intention to rent a car. Ideally she will be able to save you those additional expenses by having you stay with her and picking you up at the airport. Your presence will certainly make things easier for her when she puts the stud with Throck.

"And if I can't get the time off work?"

Well, for one thing, you have your first taste of what will soon become more and more of a problem. Not all the time, but often, the breeding program demands a full-time person. Unless you are able to take off whenever you wish for as long as you wish, the time will soon come when you may have to face the prospect of giving your full attention to the kennel. Either that, or hiring someone.

For now, however, you still have alternatives. Frozen or fresh cooled semen, for two. We will discuss those possibilities at greater length in a moment, but keep in mind that you still have an escape hatch.

NATURAL BREEDING

We shall discuss the frozen and fresh cooled semen options after natural breeding, but we do not really recommend their use to the novice breeder.

The novice should experience a natural breeding and its aftermath first. It certainly would not do to use the fresh cooled or frozen semen when breeding your own studs to your own bitches, or those who live nearby. A breeder needs to know his business from the basics up. Natural breeding is about as basic as it gets.

Lynnedora did a good job. She checked Throck's vaginal area every day for two weeks prior to her estimated due date. The estimated due date, based on past history, came and went. A week, two, then three passed. Lynnedora's chin rested on her shoes until she saw that first sign of swelling in the vulva. Bitches are seldom models of consistency when it comes to heat cycles. Six to eight months between is common.

She medicated Throck against vaginal infection, marked her calendar, called Pedunk's mother, and then called the vet, preparing him to take vaginal smears and to conduct progesterone tests.

Next she called us with the good news and a report of what she had accomplished. We found no fault. We do not use vaginal smears to predict ovulation, but there are many who swear by them. The vet can see a change in the cell shape near ovulation and signal the best time. The progesterone test also predicts. It looks for the estrogen surge that precedes ovulation.

We may become converts to these tests once Mister Moe leaves us. Right now, Mister Moe is our live-in, never-fail, forecaster. Our oldest stud dog, he can pick out a bitch in heat her first day. When she starts getting close, he urinates in her crate or near her run. Figure two more days. On the first day that she is ready, Mister Moe stops eating, camps as close to the bitch's quarters as he can get, and breathes heavily. An occasional howl is not unusual.

Visitors laugh at Mister Moe's antics. So do we. But we would gladly have our other studs follow suit. Mister Moe never misses. We are so confident of his unerring ways that we loaned him to Lynnedora as a source of second opinion.

Since we cannot lend Mister Moe to everyone, the reader should be aware there are some other indicators. If you are sure you picked up the first day, it is common to expect ovulation on the tenth to fourteenth day following. It is not a must, but common. Few are earlier; many are later.

If the time is right, the color of the discharge should change from red to clear. Use your hand to apply a little pressure near the base of her tail. The tail should swing to the side, revealing the vulva and inviting entry. If she braces those back legs in anticipation, the time has arrived, give or take a little. The stud lets you know how accurate you were. Smears, progesterone tests, retired studs, clues—what more could you ask.

Ideally, one of your indicators will put you on the plane at least a day before she's ready to accept a male. Two days are better yet — one to fly and one to rest and play. If one day is the best you can do, try mating her as late the following day as is convenient.

When the time finally arrives for Throck, Lynnedora will be in for some surprises. If she thinks that stud and bitch will just play out their roles without human assistance, she may be in for a shock. Hopefully, at least the stud will have experience.

We prefer to give the animals an opportunity to mate naturally. If all goes well, it is only for us to help the male turn during the tie and to mark the calendar.

Unfortunately, there are too many times when it doesn't happen naturally. Sometimes that's our fault. We want them to perform at our convenience before an audience. If we just put them out together and walked away, it could be that it would all work out without us. But we can't have that. We call ourselves the breeders and we want to feel important too.

We would be very happy to leave it to the animals. But many breeders are not. They are unwilling to accept a definition of breeder that limits them to the proper selection of mates, providing the ways and means, and raising the offspring. They feel they must supervise and manipulate every step in the cycle. Be the overprotective parents!

We understand the desire to feel needed and the equally intense desire to assure success for all concerned. We even applaud them. The only point we wish to make is that it may not all be necessary. Be totally prepared for anything, know how to interfere in everything, but first give the animals a chance.

In order to expose Lynnedora to as much as possible, we shall assume that the breeders gave Pedunk and Throck time, but Throck refused all of Pedunk's attempts to mount. She took special exception to rear mounting and almost took off his face.

People find it strange that a stud, most often a first-time stud, does not know what to do. More correctly, he does not know where to do. We think many of these people forget their own youth. If human children with their advanced minds require sex education courses, then certainly a stud has the right to ask for a little help finding what he knows is there somewhere.

As to the bitch, if all the indicators are positive, give the vulva a final check. It should be very swollen, soft at top and bottom, and pliable. Aggressive behavior, such as trying to bite off the stud's face, can be an indicator that she is not quite, or just past, ready. It could also mean she just does not like him. For the safety of both animals and people, muzzle the bitch with the lead. If she acts disinterested and frigid, it could be that she is just too attached to her owner. The owner should try leaving the room for a time.

The size of the breed will in large part dictate the maximum number of helpers who may be necessary and any other special conditions. One person can usually give all the necessary assistance to the toys. The medium breeds, up to eighty pounds, do well with two humans. It takes three to handle the big guys.

There is nothing very mystical about what is supposed to happen. As with human procreation, the male penis has to penetrate the vaginal area of the female in order to deposit sperm. Since the animals, like humans, are not always of equal size, one or more of the helpers may have to boost one or the other of the animals to improve the alignment. A random supply of hard-covered books serves well to sustain the animal in its elevated position after the adjustment.

A major difference between man and dog is the structure of the penis. The dog's contains bone and a large bulb at the base that swells upon penetration. The bitch's vaginal muscles then contract behind the bulb and we have what is called a tie. If the bulb swells before entry, we have an outside tie.

The duty of the person or persons assisting the bitch is to make sure the bitch does not bite, pull forward, or sit down. A hand, knee, or joined hands under the bitch's stomach can keep the bitch elevated.

The person assisting the stud helps aim, then boosts if the stud is a little short-legged. Providing the stud with a non-skid surface will help him keep his traction. In case of an outside tie, a handler should grab the rear legs of the female and prevent the male from withdrawing until it is certain the stud has completed all three phases of the ejaculation.

If all goes well and there is a tie, the work is almost over. The male will want to dismount, but the penis will remain tied. Help him either to stand down beside the bitch, or to turn tail to tail, whatever he prefers.

Ten minutes, fifteen, an hour, more — there is no telling how long it will be before the male withdraws. Keep them both as passive and immobile as you can to prevent injury to either party.

Once the withdrawal takes place, the bitch needs to go into her crate for two hours or more. Especially avoid allowing her to urinate.

Check the male to make sure the penis immediately returns to the sheath. If not, dunk the penis in a glass of cold water to stimulate retraction. Failing with that, wrap the penis in cold compresses or apply liberal amounts of K-Y lubricating jelly. Do not allow the penis to dry or the male will suffer much, much pain.

ARTIFICIAL INSEMINATION

One good tie does not necessarily result in a pregnancy. We like to see our bitches covered three times in a four-day period.

"But what if the animals refuse to cooperate?"

That happens. Often! It also happens that the owners cannot afford to get together the principals in the scenario. On occasion, there is no prospect of a natural breeding because the stud that would most help the bitch is dead.

If both parties are present, it is a rather simple matter to artificially inseminate. It is not, however, an easy process to explain. We will attempt to do just that, but we strongly urge you to watch a vet or experienced breeder before trying it yourself.

First equip yourself with a pipette that approximates the length of distance from vulva to the cervix. You will also need a syringe that fits the pipette and offers enough capacity to handle the quantity of ejaculate usually collected from your breed. Finally, you will need a plastic glass, light enough to respond to the warmth of your hand.

Keep the bitch close, stimulating the stud with her special scents. Place a hand on the sheath and gently pressure the area behind the glans penis, the bulb at the penis's base. As he starts to swell, ease back the sheath so that the penis emerges.

With one hand, continue a gentle manipulation. Cup the other hand around the glass bottom and hold the glass over the end of the penis. Stay alert. Do not miss any of the ejaculate once he starts. Also do not allow him to bruise the penis on the glass.

Many people botch the process with the next step. And the next step is the easiest step. Patience! Wait until the ejaculate goes from clear to cloudy to clear again. Three phases.

Once he finishes, work quickly and smoothly, without frenzy. Keeping the ejaculate warm with one hand, fill the syringe almost to the top, leaving only a small air pocket to propel the ejaculate.

Attach the syringe to the pipette, which has been lubricated with the K-Y jelly, and gently and carefully insert. It is especially this phase where one profits from expert training. Work the pipette slowly upward, then over the hump and downward on a diagonal toward the cervix. Never, ever, never force the pipette. If the slow and easy insertion does not glide smoothly, pull it out and start again.

Push the plunger once you have the pipette inserted. When the syringe is empty, slowly and smoothly retract the pipette and lay it aside.

Next, lift the bitch's rear so that only her front feet remain on the floor. Massage her abdomen. Your goals are two. You want gravity and the bitch's pelvic contractions to assure the sperm complete their journey.

Make sure the stud is back in his sheath, the bitch is in her crate, and your equipment is cleaned. You are finished, until the next time.

Fresh Cooled and Frozen Semen

When circumstances prevent the geographical coming together of the critters, call A.K.C. for the numbers of some of those who can furnish the kits and the ways and means of handling fresh cooled extended semen. Essentially, the stud owner will have her vet collect and cool the semen to prescribed temperatures, then ship it to your vet for insemination.

The problems arise in the transport. Do not do it over a weekend. None of the delivery services is dependable on the weekend. You can fly it in, air express, but the timing is delicate.

We tried extended semen only once and were not successful. That is not a condemnation of the system. Without hesitation, we would try again. Next time, though, we will arrange our transport well in advance and try to cover all contingencies.

As we mentioned earlier, there are certain studs who add so many positives to their progeny that we are reluctant to lose that potential when they get ready to leave us. The option exists to have their semen frozen and preserved and be used long after their time with us. The glitch — most of the owners who have semen frozen do so for their own use only.

If you know that frozen semen is available and feel that stud would contribute to what you wish to accomplish, contact the semen owner. That may or may not be the same person who last owned the animal.

Also, write to A.K.C. As you might suspect, they have rules governing the use of frozen semen. Make sure that any transactions you arrange are in compliance with those rules.

For Lynnedora and especially for Throck the deed is done and they can return home. No hurry! The longer Lynnedora can delay, the less stress will be on Throck. But time constraints may force you to leave soon. Even understanding employers and families will get strained after six days.

Those of you who ship animals should do so on the third day, or as close to then as you can. That gets the girl to the breeder a week in advance of the common ovulation interval, the tenth to fourteenth day. You should then request the breeder to keep her a week after breeding before shipping her home.

4.

Whelping

Whelping is a time to wonder and a time to hope. Although everything appeared to go well for Pedunk and Throck, there is no certainty that babies, if there are any, will ever hit the ground.

WAITING FOR THE RESULTS _____

The anxious period lasts for nearly four weeks. The vet will then palpate her, which is simply an exterior examination of the uterus. If he feels little golf balls, smile. If he doesn't, worry, but do not give up. Vets make mistakes too. Not often, but they do. While you are sweating out that first four weeks, remain optimistic.

We always assume she is, until we know she is not. One thing you can do while you are waiting is to recheck the food you are feeding her. Make sure the container proclaims AAFCO (American Association of Feed Control Officials) certification for gestation (the period you are in), lactation (the milk phase), and growth. If they have that certification, they will surely advertise it.

You might want to boost that dry menu by adding some corn oil, which we do on a regular basis in any event. Two teaspoons will give her 90-100 extra kcals and some B vitamins.

If yours is a "complete food," meaning AAFCO certified, resist other supplements, especially calcium. Calcium must be added in proper ratio with phosphorus. Too much calcium in excess of phosphorus can cause a decreased secretion of the parathyroid gland that regulates blood calcium levels. The result can be eclampsia (Milk Fever, Puerperal Tetany), a potentially life-threatening situation. Watch toy breeds for this especially.

Pregnancy is not an excuse for lethargy. Throck can still go out for walks and play. She *should* still go out for walks and play. Use good sense with her. Pregnant ladies do not react well to heat, stairs, being lifted, jumping, being chilled, or anything in excess. Shorten play periods and walks, but by no means eliminate them.

WHY A MATING COULD FAIL

If you anticipate many of the possibilities of what could have gone wrong, you can negate them. Timing causes a large percentage of the failures. Or maybe we should say lack of timing. Many keep poor records or no records at all. When they notice the bitch is messy, or dripping red, they realize she is in heat and start counting. How accurate the count is, is anybody's guess.

Then, too, a busy stud owner can ruin the timing. They receive the bitch, have their stud cover once, then ship her back.

Even if you forgo the smears and progesterone tests, a little accurate recordkeeping and watchful diligence will keep you within the time parameters. And if you do rely on smears and progesterone tests, keep the records and maintain diligence anyway. Progesterone tests are not a guarantee of successful breeding. Our observations lead us to believe that even tested bitches fail to conceive an alarmingly high percentage of the time.

"If there is a surge of estrogen, why wouldn't the tests be almost perfect in predicting ovulation?"

We have every reason to believe those who tell us that the progesterone levels approach 5 nanograms/ml at time of ovulation. Nor do we doubt a professional's ability to test and measure.

The conclusion we must then draw is that there are other reasons that a mating fails. Thus a progesterone test may improve timing, especially when confirmed by the changing cells observed in the smears, but that is only part of the problem.

Sperm count, quality, and motility can also be a part of the problem. Be concerned about the stud who has not been used in the recent past. If he is tested just before breeding your bitch, there should be no problem. If not, ask the owner to collect one time. Often that first ejaculate, after several weeks, or months, will be yellowed and of low quality and not worth wasting a breeding on.

Too, the bitch can be suffering from low grade vaginal infections that will destroy the sperm. She may also be experiencing hormonal imbalances that only the vet should attempt to remedy. If you have eliminated all the problems that are within your power to eliminate and the bitch still fails to conceive, we would certainly recommend you have her hormonal balances checked.

We are convinced that stress rivals timing as the leading enemy to conception. You and your family love your bitch and allow her to love you, day in and day out. You exercise together and play together. Someone in the family feeds her and everybody makes a big fuss on show day. Suddenly you push her into a crate and fly her off to a stranger, where a strange male mauls her. Why shouldn't she be stressed?

Think! Make it as easy for her as you possibly can. If adjustments are necessary, give her the maximum time possible to make those adjustments. You and the family have done your best to make her a person and a member of the family. Do not expect her to become an animal again overnight, just because it will be convenient for you.

PREGNANCY

Do not start counting the puppies yet. Probably everything will go just fine, but there are still five weeks of gestation. A lot can happen.

"I would rather not ask. But what should I be on the watch for?"

First let's talk about positive things you can do to help. In the next week or so, you might want to increase her food ration by ten percent. That means the exercise is even more important. Fat, at this stage, she does not need.

Avoid chills. Keep her out of the rain, unless you dry her completely when you bring her in. Extend that warning to baths. A daily brushing or two should keep her clean enough to make a bath unnecessary. But if a bath, for whatever reason, becomes an absolute must, dry her as thoroughly as you can, then keep her in a warm place until that last dampness disappears.

Do not medicate her or treat her with anti-flea preparations, under any circumstances, without first consulting with your vet. Many of these products can transfer through the placenta and cause birth defects or death.

And after you have taken all those precautions, cross your fingers. A sudden stress or trauma can cause the bitch to resorb the litter. The puppies are there and then they are gone. As we mentioned in *The Road to Westminster*, Tina lost a litter because we continued to show her. They were there and then gone.

Hopefully, the only stress Throck will have to endure is the stress of being loved too much and getting too much attention. In between pamperings, though, you should think about getting your whelping box built.

BUILDING THE WHELPING BOX

"My whelping box? I don't even know what it is, let alone how to build it."

The completed whelping box waiting for occupancy.

It is literally a box, or nest if you will, where Throck can feel secluded and safe while she delivers her puppies. It is also the place where the puppies will spend their first month or so in warmth and safety, receiving constant attention from Mom.

With a few basic tools and materials that can be purchased from any lumber yard, anyone can build a suitable whelping box. We will describe how to build one for an average Clumber. For those animals considerably larger or smaller than a Clumber you need only modify the size of the box accordingly.

Other materials may be substituted for those we suggest, with one warning. Do not build your whelping box to withstand a bombing and weigh a thousand pounds. If you stay in breeding, you will assemble and disassemble the box time after time in order to store it. Believe us, the box will get heavier with every year older you get.

Before making any purchases, we have to measure the animal that is going to use the box. Have Throck lie on her stomach, feet extended front and rear. We will want to provide that much space in the open area of the box, rounded to the nearest half foot. Throck, for example, is three feet, two inches from front toes to rear toes. To make construction easier, we will round to an even three feet and use that as the key measurement. (For those with larger or smaller animals, the key measurement equates with the size of your animal, measured in like fashion.)

One more easy calculation. A function of the box is to provide an open area where Mom can stretch out and attend to her babies. An equally important function of the box is to provide a six-inch safety zone, around the box, for the babies. When Mom walks, rolls, or changes position, there has to be an area where babies can scamper out of danger. And there is danger. More than one baby has been lost to a rolling mother or a misplaced foot.

To provide for these two functions of the box, we need only add one foot (six inches on each side) to Throck's three foot length. Four feet, then, becomes the new key figure; i.e., Throck's prone length added to the safety zone.

Supplies

Based upon the key measurement — a measurement, remember, that will vary from breed to breed — the following is a list of necessary materials:

2 – 1" x 4" x 8' boards (pine will do)
4 – 4' x 8' sheets of plywood or particle board
7 – 2" x 4" x 8' boards (buy only 2 if your box will be in living area of the house)
24 – 12" x 12" peel and stick tiles (although you will need only 16, we urge you
    to buy 24, giving you 8 to replace damaged tiles over the years)
8 – ½" wood screws
4 – 2 ½" bolts with washers and nuts
8 – 3" 'L' brackets with screws
2 – 2" cabinet door hinges
1 – hook and eye

There are lumber yards that will, for a nominal fee, cut your purchases to prescribed dimensions. Since that service is becoming more and more difficult to find, we will do all the work ourselves. Toward that end, we recommend the following list of tools:

1 – electric hand drill, with bits
1 – measuring device (tape, ruler, etc.)
1 – pair of pliers
1 – pencil
1 – saw (circular, saber, or hand)
1 – screwdriver

Tools assembled and purchases made, you should do some labeling that will help to communicate the various steps. Mark one sheet of plywood with a large "F" and the other with a large "S". Next, identify both the 1" x 4" boards with an "R". Finally, mark any two of the 2" x 4" boards with a "P" and put the rest aside for the moment.

Floor

Let's begin by selecting the sheet of plywood marked "F", for floor. Now 4' x 8', cut the sheet in half to arrive at two 4' x 4' pieces. One of the pieces is excess. We suggest you store it carefully. If the occasion ever arises that you find yourself with two pregnant bitches at the same time, you will have the floor for the second box, cut and ready to use.

Lay the piece you elected to use for this box on the floor. Count out sixteen of the tiles, then grab your rule and pencil. You want to avoid using a corner of the flooring or an edge of the board as a guide for the placement of the first tile. Often times neither the factory edge nor the side you cut is straight enough to use as a guide.

The correct way to proceed is to measure across all four sides of the floor, corner to corner, marking the exact center of each side with a slash. Using one of the "S" boards as a straight-edge, draw lines connecting the slashes from top to bottom and side to side. You will now have a large cross. Peel the paper from the first tile and lay a tile into a corner where the lines intersect in the center of the floor. If you have the tile lined up correctly, one edge will fit snug against the line you drew from top to bottom and a perpendicular edge will fit against the line from side to side.

Once that first tile is in place, the rest are easy to position. Do not be concerned if the last full tile on any side does not cover all the way to the edge. The sides sit on top of this floor and will cover any slight deficiency. If the last full tile extends slightly past the edge of the floor, simply trim the excess with shears or a craft knife.

The floor is now complete. All the breeder need decide is where to put it. Think about ease of access for the people, quiet for the mother, and controlled temperature conditions for the babies. If you select a place in the living area of your house for the box, just move your floor to that area and move on to the next phase of the box construction. If, however, you choose to locate your box in a garage, laundry room, or basement, there is an intermediate step.

Drafts are dangerous. So are chill and dampness from the floor. If you choose a location out of the warm living area, you will need those five extra 2" x 4" boards. Cut them in half and space them roughly six inches apart over the area where you plan to settle the box. You are making a platform for the floor to rest on, a good inch and a half off the floor. Do *not* get energetic and nail the floor to the platform. True, nailing would improve the structural stability. Nailing would also make those 2" x 4" boards a permanent part of the floor. Floor with tile is difficult enough to move into storage, without adding on the platform.

The Sides to the Box

Lay the sheet of plywood marked "S" flat on the floor. The sides need to be high enough to deflect drafts well over the prone mother and her babies. A foot high works; two feet high works even better. We will plan for walls that are two feet high.

Start by stretching your tape measure along the left side of the sheet of plywood, from top to bottom. Mark the plywood at two feet, four feet, six feet, and eight feet. Now do the same on the right side. Draw lines across the marks to connect them, dividing the full sheet into four equal sections, each 4' wide by 2' high.

Warm up the saw again and cut along the lines you have drawn. When that task is completed, label the pieces S-1, S-2, S-3, and S-4. While the saw is still warm, cut one inch off the four foot width of S-1 and S-3, producing pieces that are now 3'11" wide by 2' high.

Before you put the saw away, apply it to the 2" x 4" boards marked "P". The first should be cut into three pieces — two pieces 2' long and one piece 3' long (with one foot left as a scrap). From the second board cut another 3' long piece. Store the remaining 5' with your extra floor for a head start on a second box. Mark the 3' pieces P-1 and P-3. The 2' pieces should be labelled P-2 and P-4.

If all went well, you should now have four piles of pieces. The first should contain two pieces of plywood, each 2' x 3'11", S-1 and S-3. The second pile has plywood pieces S-2 and S-4. The third pile has P-1 and P-3, the 3' long pieces. In the fourth pile are P-2 and P-4, each 2' long.

To finish the sides you will need to add to those piles your bolts and woodscrews. You will also need your pencil and rule, the drill and bits, the screwdriver, and the pliers.

Lay S-1 on the floor. Measure and mark off with the pencil 1 ½" from each end. Measure off S-3 in the same manner. Turn both pieces of plywood over. Now measure in the same manner, except mark off ³/₄". In addition, use your pencil to divide each line into thirds, using a cross-hatch on the line. The cross-hatches should appear at 8" and 16" from the top along each drawn line.

With your drill and a drill bit smaller in diameter than your wood screws, drill holes through the plywood at each cross-hatch. Keep the drill handy and stand S-1 on its edge. Place the narrow side of the length of P-1 against the plywood on the side that you marked off 1 ½" from the end. The end of the plywood should be flush with the wide side of the 2" x 4", forming a perfect right angle. Drill through the same holes you did before, continuing through P-1. Attach P-1 to the plywood with two wood screws.

Move to the other end of S-1 and attach P-2. You may wonder why one end has a post that ends at the top of the plywood, while the post at the other end extends a foot above the plywood. There is a reason. The longer posts are so that you can mount a heat lamp or other such device should cold temperatures threaten the litter.

Side S-1 should stand by itself now. Use it as a pattern and complete side S-3 in the same way. Only two cautions. Remember that the posts must all be inside the box. If you left S-1 standing, you should be looking at those posts as you fasten the new posts. Also, if P-1 is to your right as you look across, P-3 should be to your left. We want the long posts to be diagonally across from each other.

At this juncture, side one and side three should be standing opposite one another, to your left and to your right. What we need to accomplish next is to complete the square by fastening the other two sides. It is an easy task since we need only set them in place, snug against the wider sides of the 2" x 4" boards and flush with the plywood sides standing ready.

What we do not want to do is fasten these last two sides to the 2" x 4" boards with wood screws, as we did the other two sides. To do so would make it more difficult to disassemble and reassemble the box over the years. Also, the holes would wear and enlarge with use. Instead, we will fasten these last two sides with bolts.

As before, we need to draw lines with cross hatches to establish our drilling points. This time, measure in from the ends of the two unattached sides 1 3/4", then draw a line from top to bottom. Place your cross hatches at 8" and 16" from the top.

Put the first of the unattached sides in position. Using the drill and a bit that is at least as large in diameter as the bolts, drill holes at the intersection of your cross hatches and the drawn lines, continuing through the plywood and the 2" x 4".

There is nothing complicated about inserting the bolts. The only caution is to avoid having the dangerous bolt ends inside the box. Insert the bolt through the 2" x 4" first. Once the bolt head is flush against the 2" x 4" and the end has passed through the plywood, add the washer and finally the nut. Tighten!

Having practiced on one, stop. Remove the bolt again. There is another step to be completed, which is more easily accomplished before the pieces are bolted together. Let's look at what we have. The tiled floor of the box lies waiting. In front of us, though still unbolted, are the four sides. They will ultimately sit on top of the floor, around its perimeter. Should we place it there, bolted and as is, we would soon notice two problems. First, Mama dog would have to jump a two-foot wall every time she wanted to get in or out. The babies would have to remain in the box until they grew legs strong enough to propel them over the sides. Second, there is no safety zone for the puppies. When Mama walks and moves, there is no place for the puppies to scamper. We can solve both problems with relative ease.

A Safety Zone

The safety zone is made by equipping the box with a pig-rail. A pig-rail is simply a shelf that hangs on the sides, under which the puppies can lie and avoid Mama.

For this construction you will need your pencil, rule, drill, and saw. You will also need the boards marked "R", the L-brackets with screws, and a screwdriver. Believe us, all those tools and supplies make the task appear more ominous that it is.

Lay all four sides flat on the floor with outsides down. Now take your pencil and rule and move into the center. The edges of the sides nearest you are the bottom edges. On each side piece, draw a horizontal line 4" up from the bottom of the board. Now measure in from the end of each side and mark a crosshatch at 1' and at 3'. These marks indicate where you want to install the L-braces.

When positioned correctly, one leg of the bracket will lie flat against the side and the other will extend up toward the installer. The top surface of that second leg should be even with the line you drew the length of the side. To check yourself, stand one of the sides up for a moment. The leg that was extending toward you should now be parallel to the floor, ready to provide bottom support for a shelf.

The brackets almost install themselves. Hold each in place against the sides and stick your pencil through the holes on the bracket to mark where you want them. Use your drill and a small bit to drill a starter hole in the center of each of those circles. Now arm yourself with a screwdriver and attach the brackets.

Now the rails. They are easier to install than the brackets. Measure the distance between the 2" x 4" boards on S-1 and S-3. Next from the 1" x 4" cut two rails 44" long and fasten them to the brackets on S-1 and S-3. Next cut two rails that are 40" long. Fasten to the brackets on S-2 and S-4. (For those who are more comfortable with carpentry, the pig-rails can be notched around the posts.) The rails are now installed and the problem of sanctuary is resolved.

The Door

Only one problem, that concerning an access, remains. Construction of a door could not be simpler, and we can offer you two choices. If you are satisfied with a permanent opening, do the following. Situate yourself facing the inside of whichever side you think would make the best front side for the whelping box. Use your rule to find the exact horizontal center of that side and make a mark. Now measure 9" to the left of center and the same to the right of center, marking both points. Through these points draw vertical lines that extend from the top of the pig-rail to the top edge of the side.

Saw through the vertical lines until you reach the pig-rail. Now rest your pencil on the pig-rail and draw a horizontal line from saw score to saw score. Saw through that line. You should now be able to lift out the 18"-wide rectangle. Mama and puppies now have access to the box.

If you wish to provide a door that can be closed to keep the puppies in the box, we can do that too. Place the rectangle you removed flat on the floor. On one side, roughly 5" from the top and 5" from the bottom, attach the hinges purchased earlier. Across the width from the hinges, an inch in from the edge, screw in the hook.

When you return the rectangle to the opening, rest the bottom on some sort of shims. Wooden matches will do, or a piece of corrugated cardboard. The object is to create a small space under the door to prevent it rubbing every time it opens and closes.

The end is near. With the rectangle resting on the shims, fasten the other halves of the hinges to the stationary side. Next, extend the hook to locate the best position for the eye. Install.

Test the hook and eye to make sure they connect properly. Remove the shims to assure the door swings freely.

A final step. Lift or slide the sides onto the floor and fasten the bolts. You have just built a whelping box.

SUPPLIES FOR THE WHELPING BOX

In addition to the box itself, you will want to get together a few more items that can make the delivery go easier for bitch, puppies, and owners. Many of them you probably already have about the house. Gather them together in an area near the whelping box. You won't want to take the time to hunt down these items once the puppies start appearing.

First give some thought to the newly constructed whelping box and its location. During the delivery, and for a month after, the box must be positioned so that you have easy access. At the same time, you must be able to restrict the bitch's movements and isolate her from curious pets, children, and visitors.

No matter where you situate the box, you must surround it with a barrier. Putting the box in a corner allows you to use two walls as half of your barrier. A 3'- or 4'-high exercise pen can make up the other half. If you do not own one of those, build a barrier. Make a frame to the desired height and cover it with 2" x 4" mesh fencing. Remember, you will have to go in and out of this compound many times, and so will the bitch. You will have to hinge a gate if you build your own barrier.

You tiled the floor of the whelping box so that the floor would be easy to clean. It is a good move, but it will prove too slippery a surface for puppies. Collect newspapers to cover the floor during delivery, and old blankets or better yet, towels, for the weeks following.

Buy at least two hot water bottles to supplement the temperature in the whelping box. A winter litter may require a larger supplement of heat than the hot water bottles can supply. Avoid heating pads. They can dehydrate puppies. Instead, attach heat lamps to the long corner posts. Make sure you have an outlet available.

Find a sturdy cardboard box. For now, furnish it with its own hot water bottle and two bath towels. While on the subject of towels, prepare a pile of a half dozen, minimum.

The following is a list of miscellaneous items you will need:

White thread or unwaxed dental floss	Two or three green trash bags
	Rectal thermometer
Two pairs of forceps	Scissors
Baby scale	Alcohol
Pen and pad	Cotton balls
A box of white plastic kitchen garbage bags	

You probably have most of those items around the house already. But around the house isn't good enough. Now, while you have time, collect the items into a delivery kit that will be easily accessible when the time comes.

Delivery supplies: scale for weighing newborns; newspaper for cleanup and discarding placentas; clean towels for drying newborns as well as rubbing to stimulate breathing; white thread for tying the umbilical cord; scissors for cutting the umbilical cord; forceps for clamping the umbilical cord prior to tying and cutting it off.

THE DUE DATE

"How do we know when it's time? Will Throck warn us?"

Not necessarily! Some bitches read the book and follow the script perfectly. Other bitches — most of them, probably — flex the rules and stray. You would not be the first breeder to awaken in the morning to puppies in progress, or the first to return home from work to a protesting litter.

It is supposed to be sixty-three days from the breeding date, but you don't know on which day Throck conceived. What if Throck did not conceive until the second try, or the third?

There is a safer way. Two weeks, give or take a few days, before the supposed date, start charting Throck's temperature. Take a reading at night and in the morning, as close to twelve hours apart as is convenient. Chart the results.

For most of the two weeks, her temperature will hover between 101° F and 102° F. If the readings indicate a temperature far above or below that range, be concerned. If the situation persists, consult your vet.

You should call the vet in any event to remind him how close Throck is. If he cannot be available to give you emergency assistance, he will surely have another vet on call.

LABOR

At sixty-three days from the date of conception, give or take a little, Throck's temperature will take a perceptible dip to 99° F or lower. Let's assume you take the temperature in the morning and read 99.5° F. Is she on her way down, or did she bottom out during the night and start up again? Take a second reading an hour after the first and you can then calculate her status. As a rule, within twenty-four hours of the time the temperature reaches its lowest point, labor will start.

The next few hours are confusing for the bitch and nervewracking for the owners. Do what you can to distract yourself. Put the bitch into the whelping box and talk to her. (You should introduce her to the box a week early. Each day put her in and sit nearby. Talk to her.) Help her to understand the rest is reserved to her.

Throck will probably lie in a fully stretched position, head between her front feet. Pathetic glances will twist your heart and there will be outbursts of panting.

She won't hold that or any position very long. She will appear restless, dig at the newspapers, and show concern for her vaginal area.

A mother-in-waiting. The early stages of labor have commenced; note the pathetic expression.

She will lick and lick and even insist on going out to urinate. Do not let her go out alone. Go with her and stay close. If she only urinates, back to the whelping box you go.

You and Throck may well repeat the sequence several times, until one time, inside or outside, a bubble of membrane will bulge from the vulva. Do not touch it. You are seeing the water sac. Throck will break it, soaking herself and the area around her.

"How can I help her?"

One of us usually sits on the floor next to the whelping box once the water breaks and the contractions start. If the water breaks in the box, clean out the wet newspapers and replace them. There will soon be enough mess, so you don't want to start in one.

While the contractions course through Throck's body, there is little for you to do beyond reassuring her with a calm voice and an occasional pat. Write down the time she starts and wait.

Throck may insist on going out again. Try to change her mind. If she persists, grab a towel and go with her. She may be confusing an impending delivery with the need to eliminate waste. If it is dark and you must go out, take a flashlight, preferably a lantern type that you can set on the ground and thus free your hands.

THE BIRTH

Whether inside or out, you will eventually see another bubble protrude from the vulva. It will grow, then out slides a puppy in a bag.

With the second contraction, half the puppy is delivered.

Within moments the placenta, attached to the sack by the umbilical cord, will follow.

At this point, you have choices. There are several things that have to happen. The cord must be severed, the sack opened, the puppy's lungs and nose cleared of mucus, the placenta disposed of, and the baby must ingest a squirt or three of mother's milk.

Some breeders let Mom do everything, even absenting themselves during the delivery period. Mom severs the cord with her teeth, chews open the bag, licks away the mucus, consumes the placenta, and cleans and feeds the baby. All the owner has to do is count the survivors at the end.

No, that's not quite all. There are those owners who, when presented with a large litter, believe in culling immediately. They separate the litter into halves and destroy the fifty percent they consider inferior.

We, on the other hand, neither leave it to Mom nor cull litters. We prefer to interfere. We do so to avoid accidents, assure consistency, and relieve the bitch of the additional responsibilities.

TENDING TO THE PUPPIES

As soon as baby and placenta are free of the mother, one of us rips open the sack and frees the puppy's nose. The other applies one pair of forceps to the placenta end of the cord and one pair to the puppy end. That person, in spite of slippery hands, then uses the thread to tie a tight knot around the section between the forceps. Using the scissors, the cord is then cut on the placenta side of the knot.

As soon as the cord is cut, the person who opened the sack lifts the puppy over his head with both hands. The hands and puppy, nose first, then swing down to a position between the holder's knees, from twelve o'clock counterclockwise to six o'clock, say. The object is to clear the mucus from puppy's nose and lungs.

Then lay the puppy in a towel and briskly dry it down. Massage the whole body. You are warming the puppy and stimulating breathing. The other person wraps the placenta in newspaper and tosses it in the garbage. There are those who believe the bitch should be allowed to eat the placentas as a source of protein and strength. We have never seen a reliable confirmation of that theory. We do know they lend to vomiting and diarrhea. We are careful to count them — one placenta for each puppy — to be certain they are all delivered, but our bitches only get a taste if we are careless.

Before returning the puppy to its mother, weigh it and record any distinguishing marks. Look carefully. It is often difficult to pick up markings on a wet pup. Remove any soiled newspapers from the box and put down clean papers.

The mother may not be satisfied with your cleaning and may want to use that big tongue to follow up. Let her. With luck she will poop the pup. Though the procedure may offend the genteel, it is normal for Mom to dispose of puppy poop by eating it. The first movement is a tar-like substance. Once Mom licks it out, the eliminatory tract is open for natural defecation.

Watch until you see the puppy suckle. Those first gulps are vitally important in that they supply the puppy with colostrum, a nutritious

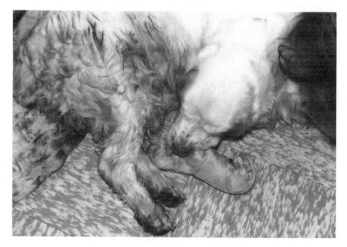

The mother immediately licks the newborn. Her knowledge of neonatal care is instinctive.

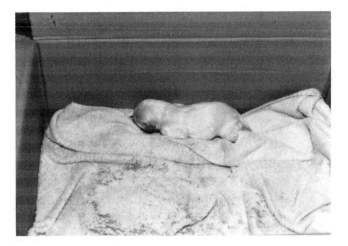

The firstborn puppy waits in a sturdy box while the mother delivers the second puppy.

liquid that also provides antibodies. These antibodies protect the puppies until they are old enough to be vaccinated.

In spite of what most people think, the puppy does not always know how to start sucking the teat. If the puppy does not catch on, gently squeeze the teat until drops form on the nipple. If the liquid is not quite the white color you expect, do not worry. Colostrum has a yellow tinge. Open the puppy's jaws and put them on the nipple. Then close the jaws and gently squeeze them and the nipple. It will only take a squeeze or two for the pup to get the idea.

This is the time to fill the hot water bottle you have provided for the puppy box. Leave the puppy with its mother until she starts contracting in preparation for the next delivery. At first sign of those contractions, remove the sucking puppy to the puppy box. In the ensuing excitement, there is no danger of the baby in the puppy box being accidentally injured. After the birth of a new puppy, put all puppies back with Mom. Remove them all to the puppy box in time for the next.

Throck may want some water between deliveries. Offer it, but do not let her drink too much.

THE TRIP TO THE VET

When you think she is through, pack the puppies into the puppy box on a towel-covered, freshly warmed, hot water bottle. Also cover the box with a towel, allowing only enough opening for fresh air. Now give Mom a quick sponge bath. Load Mom and puppies into your vehicle and take them to the vet.

Once there, the vet will check the health of the puppies. He will also examine Throck to make sure she delivered all puppies and placentas. He may well inject her with oxytocin, which stimulates the contraction of the uterus and assists her in cleaning out. The oxytocin also stimulates milk production.

When the vet pronounces Mom and puppies well, the breeder's heartbeat and breathing return to normal. If yours is a breed that docks tails, or makes other alterations, this is the time to make an appointment. Clumbers, for example, usually have their tails docked and front dewclaws removed at the age of three days. The dewclaw is the smallest claw of the animal's foot and does not touch the ground, but is in a thumb-like position. It is believed that in the wild the dewclaw was useful to the animal. Now it is considered an evolutionary relic that is useless to the animal. As the dewclaws are often pulled or cut in the brushing and grooming cycle, providing a painful potential for infection, it is to the benefit of the animal to remove them—a nearly painless procedure if done the first three or four days of life.

Exercising the same care you used in preparing for the trip in, repack the puppies. Throck is now a dam and you are now a breeder. The pups? Why, they are now hungry.

Three days old, and after the tail docking. Note the amazing growth already.

5.

Whelping Problems and Remedies

Would that nature was perfect and that whelping always went as smoothly as we described it in the previous chapter. It does not always go so smoothly. Too often, whelping can bring heartache and tears.

"If problems happen, should I call the vet?"

Sometimes and sometimes not. There may not be time to call the vet. And there are problems the owner can resolve as efficiently as the vet can. But there are occasions when the skill and knowledge of your vet are an absolute necessity, with the life of the bitch and/or the puppies in the balance.

In the previous chapter, we two-stepped through a textbook whelping. If we knew a good fairy who would grant our wishes, we would wish that all your bitches whelped as easily.

We do not know any fairies, good or bad. Therefore, we feel safe in predicting that, if you breed several litters, the time will come, perhaps come and come and come, when the whelping will present problems. You may lose your bitch, puppies, and all if you are not prepared and capable of acting immediately. Let's walk through the sequence one more time and, this time, prepare you for trouble.

FALSE PREGNANCY

Let's go back to that first four weeks after breeding. You return home after witnessing two natural breedings and an artificial insemination. In your own mind, you are certain Throck is pregnant.

Daily, the family makes a big fuss over her. You check for signs. The vulva remains soft, the nipples distend. You are positive the mammys are swelling.

The vet palpates. He could be wrong, he assures you, but he finds no puppies. He must be wrong. Throck keeps acting pregnant. Somehow she realizes the family wants her to have babies; she wants babies.

She produces milk, swells abdominally, and nests in corners and on the furniture. But there are no puppies.

Give Throck extra helpings of love. She tried for you and tried for herself. She may even go so far as to adopt a toy and treat it as her baby. You have now witnessed a false pregnancy.

TEMPERATURE DROPS TOO EARLY OR LATE __

Let's say that the pregnancy is not false. Happily, the vet confirms the good news. The nine weeks pass without incident.

Do not become complacent. As soon as Throck's temperature drops, call to confirm your vet's availability or that of his surrogate. If there are periods of time when no one can be available to help, call the most experienced breeder you know. The breed of dog does not matter. What does matter is the breeder's willingness to help in case of emergency.

"What if I don't know an experienced breeder?"

Ask your vet for a name or call the nearest Kennel Club. It may well be that you will not encounter anything out of the ordinary — so much the better. Still, knowing reinforcements are available tends to calm the nerves.

If the temperature drop occurs earlier than sixty-three days after the first breeding (the normal gestation period), the call to the vet may take on a new dimension. That does not imply panic. If the time lapse has been less than fifty-eight days, just calmly inform him that you and Throck are on your way.

Perhaps more worrisome is the bitch who passes the sixty-third day without a temperature drop. You can still put a hold on the panic. The gestation period can last as long as sixty-eight days past the final breeding. Still, alert your vet to the situation. The days past sixty-three will seem very long.

Caesarean Section

"And if she goes sixty-nine days?"

You will be at the vet's office very early in the morning. In fact the vet will very likely want to check her before that. He may well suggest a Caesarean section. That sounds worse than it is. There are breeders who have the vet deliver all their bitches by C-section. It is simply the taking of the fetuses by cutting through the walls of the abdomen and uterus.

Come to think of it, the C-section is almost as bad as it sounds. The vet may ask you to assist as he lifts the puppies from the mother. What he will hand you is a limp blob that has responded to the anesthesia given to the mother. Sometimes vigorous massage and a few drops of Dopram administered orally will bring the puppies out of their shock and start their life; sometimes it won't. Whole litters have been lost to anesthesia. At best, you will, for at least the first week, notice the difference between the activity level of those pups born before the anesthesia and those born after.

WAITING FOR DELIVERY

Even if all is well and the temperature drops on or about the sixty-third day, one of the most stressful times for owner and bitch follows the temperature move, while waiting for delivery to start. Panting, pacing, scratching — the bitch and the owner will do strange things.

Wait with her and give Throck lots of gentle praise. Instinct or not, Throck, especially if she is a maiden bitch, will be apprehensive over what is happening to her. At the very least, your praise assures her that the pack leader is pleased.

While you wait, Throck will probably stretch out full-length and look at you with eyes that ask why you allowed that stud to get her into this mess. Moments later she may jump to her feet and start nesting or lick at her vaginal area.

Watch closely. Contractions should start. When you see the first contraction, jot down the time.

What should happen next is the appearance of a balloon-like entity from the vulva. This is the water sac. Leave it alone. Throck will break it when it's time. The sac should contain an odorless, dark-green pigmented liquid. That liquid is intended to lubricate the birth canal. If the liquid should prove to be of a different color, or foul smelling, grab the phone.

Contractions will move the baby along the birth canal. Soon you should see a puppy in a sack coming out head first. Throck may choose any one of several positions, from standing to lying down, while she delivers. The important thing is not how she delivers, but that she delivers.

We get concerned if a bitch gives every indication that she is trying to deliver and does not. If she goes over an hour without results we get very concerned. The phone is in our hand at the end of two hours and we are consulting with the vet. The decision is his whether to wait or operate. At times such as these a vet more than earns his fee.

If all goes well, you can watch a puppy appear. The bitch may insist on ripping open the membranous sack that surrounds the puppy herself. Let her. But do not give her long to decide. That sack also contains amniotic fluid in which the puppy can drown.

We only allow the bitch a second or two to make her decision. Most of our bitches seem to be quite content to let us do the work. There is really not much to it. The thickness of the membrane may surprise you, but it is easily torn. Using only fingers, never instruments, rip the sack apart at the head end and free the puppy's nose.

A BROKEN SACK

Too often a puppy appears with the sack already broken. Your heart will beat faster. Stay as calm as you can. Many healthy Champions come into the world with sacks broken.

There are also those who never get the chance to experience life because they are delivered with the sack broken. To be more accurate, they smother because they spend too long in the birth canal with a broken sack and without oxygen. You will probably work to revive the beautifully formed, full-term puppy. Clear the mucus, rub the puppy briskly with a towel, even try C.P.R.

We always try those things in like situations, plus a couple more things. Try holding the puppy head down, then tail down, reversing every three seconds. The idea is to create a vacuum that pulls air into the lungs when it releases.

Time is passing and you are risking brain damage to the pup should you save it. One last try. Fill one pan with quite cold water and another with very warm water. Dunk the pup to its chin in first one and then the other. Repeat and repeat.

The puppy will certainly not live if you try nothing. Sometimes your efforts will result in life. Most often they will not. And then you will cry, just as we cry.

NO PLACENTA VISIBLE

Another problem that will make your heart race is seeing the puppy presented, with or without the sack, with the umbilical cord still firmly connected and without the placenta in sight. Sometimes the puppy just hangs, suspended in mid-air, a half-inch from the mother's vulva. Now what do you do?

What you do not do is pull on the puppy. To do so would most probably lead to the puppy having an umbilical hernia, or worse. You could disembowel the baby.

Instead, support the puppy and try to prevent her from getting a hernia from the pull of her own weight. A second person really helps in this instance. While you are tearing the sack, the second set of fingers should grasp the cord and gently pull the placenta from the bitch. Gently! All you need to gain is enough cord length to clamp, cut, and tie the cord. The bitch will expel the placenta with the next contraction.

A BLOCKAGE IN THE BIRTH CANAL

In the meantime, you have resolved one problem, just in time for the next problem. This time you are sure there is something in the canal and the bitch is straining to deliver, but there is no baby! You will worry a lot, but do not let your concern petrify you.

Scrub your index finger and remove any jewelry from that finger. If necessary, cut and emery the nail. Dip the finger in petroleum jelly, then slowly insert it into the bitch's vagina. Why not use a glove? Because you will want an unimpaired sense of touch.

There are any number of books that will describe what that finger might encounter and they will suggest manipulations to correct problems. This book will not do that. All we want that finger to discover is whether there is something or somethings in the canal. If the answer is yes and the bitch continues to strain, it is time for a call to the vet. If the vet wants you to probe further and to use that finger in an attempt to loosen a multiple pup blockage or a faulty presentation, the call is his. Let the professional guide you through it. Your luck will be better if the vet lives close and can get there quickly enough to manipulate the blockage himself.

MUMMY PUPPIES

There is nothing either you or the vet can do if the bitch presents a water puppy, or a mummy puppy. Without going into disturbing detail, these are puppies that have died during pregnancy and are in various stages of deterioration. You will recognize them. They are part of breeding. If you are still certain you want to be a breeder, you must learn to deal with each and keep moving on.

WHELPING EMERGENCIES

We separate the emergencies from the problems because the emergencies threaten the life of the bitch or puppies, or both, if not acted on immediately. Wishing will not make emergencies disappear, and an emergency is not the time to delude yourself into thinking you know as much as your vet does.

A screaming bitch, for example, moves us to the telephone every time. The first opportunity you have to hear a screaming bitch will help you understand why. By the time the conversation with the vet ends, the other of us has Throck already in the car.

Equally dangerous is the sequence that finds the water breaking, followed by involuntary contractions and voluntary straining but no puppy. An hour passes with more contractions and more straining. Still no puppy. This is a time to worry. The straining indicates a puppy has entered the birth canal. An hour is all you can afford. To wait longer jeopardizes the puppy in the canal, as well as those coming after it. The delay could exhaust the mother, who will keep trying, possibly precluding a normal delivery of those others. Some breeders wait two hours. We used to. Sometimes we do not wait an hour now.

Even if something like that happens at three in the morning, call the vet. Do not despair. This is what the vet is paid to do.

Another emergency condition occurs when the bitch gives off a yellow fluid. Start packing for a trip. If she does not deliver anything within fifteen minutes, thirty on the outside, be on your way.

Uterine Inertia

Both bitch and litter may well be in serious trouble if contractions stop and the bitch shows evidence of exhaustion. What you may be witnessing is a condition called uterine inertia. In laymen's terms, uterine inertia is a condition in which the uterus lacks the energy to continue the expulsion of fetuses. There are several possible causes. Uterine inertia can result from the effort expended trying to deliver a large puppy, too much amniotic fluid, a large litter, deficiency of oxytocin or calcium, or old-fashioned obesity and poor muscle tone.

We know breeders who keep a supply of oxytocin on hand for such situations. If the bitch appears to quit but there are still puppies to be delivered, these breeders routinely inject the bitch with a shot of oxytocin, sometimes hourly, until the rest of the puppies are delivered.

This is a very dangerous response to an emergency situation, as we see it. In the first place, oxytocin is a prescription drug and can be very dangerous. True, the uterus may respond to the oxytocin (Pitocin™) and produce strong contractions. You may be safe if that was Mom's problem. But what if that's not the problem? Suppose she needs calcium rather than oxytocin. Or worse, the problem could be a mechanical blockage. The oxytocin, in this instance, could cause uterine rupture.

Call the Vet

Emergencies are for vets. Do not take the burden of handling them on yourself. If the vet will come to you, an event that still happens on rare occasions, so much the better. Usually, however, especially if called during his office hours, the vet will ask you to bring Mom and born pups to the office. You are ready for that. If the weather is bad and it worries you to take the animals out, keep telling yourself that the vet is trained for emergencies and will better be able to react to anything with the proper instruments and medicines close to hand.

The happy result of such a trip is watching the vet assist the bitch in delivering the remainder of the litter, all healthy and eager for life. We wish that ending for all those who must face these emergencies.

There are other possibilities. The vet is well trained and very likely well experienced; but though some will argue to the contrary, they are not gods. Try as she will, employing full training and best effort, the vet cannot always prevail and produce a happy result. The unborn may never breathe life. The bitch may not survive. At least you will know you gave them the best chance possible. You saw an emergency and got them help. The rest was, for some reason, meant to be.

6.

Post-Natal Care

We hope you will emerge from the whelping experience with bitch — now dam—in good health and the litter thriving. That is not to say that we can now relax.

The twenty-four-hour-a-day vigil starts and will last for a week. Watch Mom's feet. We don't want her crushing bodies. Without meaning to, she can also cannibalize and smother. Change the hot water bottles often. Puppies, even with their mother to cuddle against, can suffer if temperatures drop below 75° F.

PREPARING THE BOX FOR PUPPIES

Mom will keep her puppies and the box as clean as she knows how, but you can help. When you return from the vet and before you return the dam's pups to her, remove the newspapers and spread towels over the floor. This will give the family a clean start and provide some traction for the puppies.

Mother and children resting comfortably.

We know breeders who prefer to cover the floor of the box with a blanket. That works too. Of course the whole blanket must be removed, washed, and dried if a small area gets soiled. Towels can be replaced piecemeal.

Certainly a blanket is better than a slippery surface. Puppies brought up on slippery surfaces risk becoming swimmers rather than walkers. Those poor swimmer puppies resemble turtles, lying on their stomaches with their legs out to the side and unable to stand. A fat puppy and/or a large-boned breed is especially at risk.

Our only concern with the use of blankets is their bulk and continuity. If a puppy whose eyes have not yet opened loses its sense of direction and winds up under the blanket, he could tire and suffocate before he finds his way out. A towel, however, is much more easily escaped.

DANGERS TO THE DAM'S HEALTH

The mistake that many breeders make during that first week is in ignoring the vulnerability of Mom. She may not appear to be as fragile as her babies, but in some ways she is even more fragile.

The ordeal of carrying and delivering a litter has taken its toll on Throck's body. The sooner we can strengthen her again, the better she will supply milk and care for her children.

We start the dam on a special diet the first feeding after whelping. To her normal ration of dry food, we add a healthy tablespoon of cottage cheese, a fried egg, and half a can of moist food. Sounds like a lot? Wait until you see how soon it disappears.

The bitch, in addition to requiring a special diet, must also be watched for any sign of eclampsia, metritis, and/or mastitis.

Eclampsia

If Mom suddenly becomes restless, starts panting excessively, and whines, check her temperature. She may be in the first stages of eclampsia, or milk fever. Her temperature could elevate to 106° F. If it is eclampsia, we are dealing with a low serum calcium level, usually caused by a malfunctioning pituitary gland. Make no mistake, the condition is life-threatening. Should the bitch stagger when she walks or lie with legs extended and appear unable to rise, she may already be in an advanced stage. Call the vet, tell him why you are coming, and hurry. Only an intravenous injection of calcium solution can save her life. At the same time, you are creating orphans in the all but technical sense. Mom will not be allowed to nurse the pups again.

Mastitis

Another problem that can beset the new mother is mastitis. This comes in varieties. Galactostasis involves caked breasts. Often the breast in question is not being adequately drained by the pups. The dam will let you know about her problem because the breast will be tender to the touch. On closer examination, you will probably find that the tender breast is also swollen, hard, and warm.

Call the vet. He may want to see Throck to satisfy himself that the situation has not progressed into Acute Septic Mastitis. If such is not the case, he will probably prescribe camphorated oil applications, hot packs, and testosterone.

With acute mastitis, the breast usually turns purplish. Throck may get restless and refuse to eat. Insert the thermometer and start dialing. If her temperature is elevated, she may have an abscess. The infection can be dangerous for Throck and fatal for sucking puppies.

Antibiotics will cure Throck. But if she is quite toxic, the puppies may have to be treated as orphans. (More on that later.)

Metritis

A less common affliction, especially if you heed our advice and take the mother for a vet check when whelping ends, is a condition called metritis. It is an infection of the uterus, caused by several things, with retained placentas and mummified fetuses leading the way.

To feel safe, take the dam's temperature every day for the first month. A temperature of 103°F and more is a concern. If she also shows a heavy, darkish discharge, refuses food, and loses interest in her pups, worry a lot. If Throck does have acute metritis, her life is in danger.

Unfortunately for everyone concerned, even if the vet saves Mom, she will probably never be able to nurse the litter again. Her milk may be toxic. Whether it's toxic or not, she will need all her strength to fight off the metritis and save her own life. Though Mom survives, her pups are now dependent on the breeder.

ORPHANED PUPPIES

Orphaned puppies, as you can imagine, are a lot of work. And the more puppies, the more work. We have talked about the importance of keeping the puppies warm. With no Mom to cuddle to, the breeder must be even more vigilant.

Without Mom, first week puppies will want the whelping box to range in temperature from 85°F to 90°F. Lower the temperature five degrees per week for the next month. With a thermometer in the box, hot water bottles under towels are still the best bet. The problem with these is at night, when the bottles must be refilled to maintain the temperature.

If someone can stay up with the puppies every evening for three or four weeks, that's wonderful. Or if there is someone who can get up to take care of the puppies every two hours, the problem eases. Lacking either option, you might want to think about a thermostatically controlled heating pad for evening use. Remember that the heat supplied by a heating pad is dry and can dehydrate the puppies. If possible, provide 55% humidity in the room. If that's not possible, only heat half of the box with the pads, allowing plenty of room for the pups to retreat should they become uncomfortable and want to cool off.

Feeding

Not having Mom also means that the breeder must take on the responsibility of feeding the litter. That task could easily qualify for the list of things that are easier said than accomplished.

First, we must choose a method — eyedropper, bottle, or tube. This is not a difficult selection. It is difficult to control the flow of fluid from an eyedropper and the decision of when to dispense is left to the breeder. A wrong decision by the breeder can send fluid into the puppy's lung rather than the stomach. The result can be pneumonia, and probably death.

A tube, when used expertly, is a far better choice. The person using the tube must make sure he inserts the tube into the stomach and does not poke on through the stomach. A vet can do that and can teach the breeder. But knowing how only makes it a little easier, especially in the middle of the night. Do you want that additional responsibility? Then use the tube.

For us, the bottle is a better choice. Most vets and many pet stores can furnish you with small animal nursers. These should have durable nipples that ooze milk when the bottle is held upside down. The fluid streams out? Discard the nipple. The fluid will not ooze out? Heat a needle and enlarge the nipple holes.

Whatever method you select, you will now have to choose the nourishment. But before we make that decision, a warning should be given. Babies must be raised in a squeaky clean environment, especially if the puppy was never fortified against disease by ingesting colostrum from Mom. Boil all utensils, scrub thoroughly before you feed, and allow no outside visitors. Change the bedding often. The vet may want to vaccinate early at three or four weeks, rather than six.

Some feed a product such as Esbilac, a simulated bitch's milk. Other breeders swear by goats' milk. And there are several home remedies. We subscribe to one of the latter—four ounces of evaporated milk, four ounces of warm water, and one teaspoon of light Karo syrup, warmed to approximately 100° F. Test it on the inside of your wrist before you offer it to the pup.

How often do you feed? We have charts that recommend 10cc (which are assumed to contain one calorie each) per pound of animal weight, distributed over four feedings. Another chart advises two teaspoons of formula per ounce of animal weight eight times per day. There are more charts.

All the charts are a little too precise for us. We feed on demand, but no more than four times a day. We lay the puppy on his belly to feed, being sure to keep the nipple full. Try pulling the nipple gently from the mouth to encourage a more energetic sucking. We offer 8cc per feeding and observe from there. Do not forget to burp each little guy before you go on to the next. You will also need to stimulate gently the anal area with a warm, moist cloth to simulate Mom's tongue and cause the baby to defecate. The same method must be exercised in the appropriate area (male or female) to stimulate urination.

Observe the Orphans

Observe! This is a must with orphan puppies. Observe their responses. If they cry all day, gain no weight, feel cool, act listless — all these signs may be due to underfeeding. Check the puppy's temperature. If the stool is soft and colored yellow to green, you may be overfeeding. Gray or white diarrhea deserves a call to the vet. A gently rounded stomach after each feeding, steady weight gain, and firm yellow stools indicate success. As long as the puppies continue to prosper, keep on what you're doing and do not change a thing.

Often when we mention stool color to first litter owners, or would-be owners, the thought of examining diarrhea wrinkles their noses. A reminder! Your involvement with feces, in various stages of solidity, will be extensive. The dam usually disposes of all such excrement and cleans the pups who wade or roll in it before she gets there. But these are orphans. You are replacing the dam. You do the cleaning, the wiping off, and the baths. Make sure you do half as thorough a job as their Mom would have.

When does it end? The cleaning declines as soon as you can teach the tykes to toddle outside. When that happens depends in large part on weather and facility. We have a doggy door that leads from the kitchen to a fenced-off puppy yard. Our puppies, orphaned or not, are out for the first time at four weeks, weather permitting. All owners will have to make that decision in terms of their facility, the size and soundness of the pups, and the weather. Toy breed puppies in an upstairs apartment during winter would put the breeder in an unenviable situation. Use the same logic and sequences mentioned in *The Road to Westminster* under housebreaking, substituting your whelping box area for the crate.

The necessity to feed will last a good while longer. At three weeks, start supplementing the bottles with a mush made from warm water and a reliable puppy food. Keep it on the soupy side. The first few days, four times a day, they will gather around and lap off the juice. Then one pup will get adventurous, and another. Once they start, gradually cut back on the liquid until you are serving the food dry. The pups will soon devour what they can reach and fight each other for the crumbs. Once you start the weaning process, it should only take two weeks, three at the most, to wean the litter from the bottle to solid food.

One caution about orphaned puppies. For your own protection, guard against forming too strong a bond. Each time you cuddle and nurture one of those babies, repeat aloud that you are raising it for someone else. A breeder cannot keep them all and continue very long as a breeder. It is difficult to part with puppies; orphans are even more difficult.

PREVENTING TRAGEDY

Worst is when you must part with a puppy lost to death. Even though the mother services and appears to take her role seriously, again we urge you to keep a constant vigil around the clock the first week of the puppies' lives. Still you may lose some. A mother's foot breaks a neck or an apparently healthy puppy stops breathing.

Keep the puppies from getting chilled. Cuddling with Mom, littermates, and hot water bottles helps. Lights and heating pads work less well, and should always be teamed with the proper humidity control.

After that, if something goes wrong, rely on your vet. With adult animals, we can often afford the luxury of waiting to see if a condition persists. You cannot do that with a puppy. Believe us when we tell you that death can result in minutes. If bad signs appear, call the vet immediately.

What are the bad signs? A list of them follows:

1. Rejection — The mother pushes the baby aside and does not want to nurse it.
2. Diarrhea — A possible indication of viral or bacterial infections.
3. Hyperactivity and Crying — Unusual in a healthy puppy, especially if that activity takes him away from dam and siblings.
4. Skin Color or Resilience Changes — Bellies should be pink. Any color other than pink can mean trouble. The skin should also be resilient. If you pucker it with your fingers and the pucker remains, the baby may well be dehydrating.
5. Nursing Stops — If the pup is just starting life, put the nipple in its mouth, work out a little milk, then ring his jaws with your fingers and gently squeeze. If the pup knows how to suck and refuses, hurry the call.
6. Chill — One puppy feels noticeably cooler than the other puppies. This condition could result from actual chill or low blood sugar. As you phone, hold the pup against the skin of your stomach and cover him with your shirt or sweater. The baby is in terrible danger if his temperature is 94° F or lower.

Most often, prompt action by you and the vet can prevent tragedy. Do not listen to baloney from answering services or well-meaning receptionists. Insist that the vet see a puppy with any of those danger signs. Right now! Moments mean lives. If the vet will not or cannot oblige, call others until one does. You may well want to consider making that latter person your permanent partner.

Do not let the puppies abuse their mother. Toenails hurt breasts and teeth brutalize nipples. Check puppies' nails and keep them trimmed. Start weaning at four or five weeks at the latest.

Fat puppies develop problems. Swimmers are most often fat puppies, as are those who ultimately will be down in the pastern. A puppy should remain on the lean side and give the bones and support system an opportunity to grow first. It may be that Mom is too generous with her milk and feeds too often. After the first two weeks, separate Mom and her charges for an hour or two at various times during the day. The pup is now limited in the quantity he can drink and soon learns to eat on schedule. No snacks are allowed.

Bloated tummies are not always due to food intake. Worms can also cause such a condition. How dangerous are worms? We have a purchased male who is blind in one eye because the breeder did not treat roundworms. Hooks and whips are worse.

Contrary to what the supermarkets would have you believe, some of the products they sell as wormers can be as dangerous to puppies as the worms, if the wormers are misused. From three weeks, take stool samples to your vet for analysis. Let the professional bear the responsibility for diagnosis and prescription.

A last caution before leaving the subject of post-natal care. Fading puppy syndrome, probably a herpes virus, can start through a litter and wipe it out, one puppy after another, in a few days. Before they die, they cry in agony and gasp for breath. Not a pretty picture is it? It will test your mettle, helplessly watching pups die. Well, there is something worse.

Cerebellar Hypoplasia

The condition is referred to as cerebellar hypoplasia. A puppy doesn't appear as coordinated as the others; legs and head tremble at times; disorientation occurs more frequently; epileptic seizures occur.

As the pup ages, the rear legs fail to respond on demand. If the baby gets up, she soon falls. Most often she cannot get up without help. She moves from one place to another by using her front legs and dragging her rear.

The vet may tell you that with love and patience she could grow out of the condition and learn to lead a reasonably normal life. And there is that chance. But the possibility is very, very, very remote.

That does not matter, you say. As a breeder, you are dedicated to giving life, not taking it. One would not destroy a child with the same malady. We will live with the mistakes as well as the triumphs.

It is noble rhetoric and well intended, but nonetheless foolhardy. With luck you will establish a communication with the puppy. She may try to walk when you help her. The baby may even drag herself to where you are sitting, nuzzle your leg, untie your shoelaces. The attachment strengthens in both directions.

The seizures come more often and she has to be medicated. Other animals run and play. She cannot. More and more frequently she loses control of bladder and bowels and lies in her own waste. No matter what you would hope to see happen, there is no way to convince yourself that she has a quality life, or ever will. Even though you give her all your free time, at the expense of both human family and other pets, you reach the point where you can no longer pretend hers is a quality existence.

If you have puppies with this condition, this one time let your head guide your heart. Let the vet put them down. It will rip out your heart. Please do it. It gets more difficult with every passing day. Save the puppy from suffering the delay.

Breeding is triumph and disaster, winners' ribbons and graves. Fortunately, there is usually more joy than pain, but a breeder must always be prepared to deal with both.

7.

Raising the Litter

Raising the litter is the fun part! The puppies may later develop health problems. Certainly you will have to sell most or all in a few weeks. For the moment, however, once the weaning is completed, those wonderful, cuddly, cute babies are all yours.

Go ahead, enjoy. We have given much ink to preparing you for the pain. This is the other side! Hug them, kiss them, get down on the floor and play games with them. The more contact they have with humans, the more they will be amenable to socialization. This is your primary job — preparing your puppies to go off and love their permanent people.

There are other obligations. Do not forget the obligation to yourself. It may be that you will turn out to be a one litter breeder. There is no dishonor in that. Many have a low threshold for pain and no amount of triumph can offset it. Rather than go through the anxiety again, some prefer to retire from breeding after that initial experience. It is better for themselves and subsequent generations of their breed that they know their limitations.

RECORDKEEPING

If, however, you intend to continue, perhaps your next most important responsibility is recordkeeping — after keeping puppies and adults healthy, then socializing the litter, of course. You may think that these babies are so precious that you will never forget a single feature on any one of them. You are wrong. Ten litters from now you will be pressed to remember how many puppies survived your first litter.

The records are for your use and the health of your breeding program. What records you keep, therefore, are your business. We do, however, have some suggestions.

Financial Records

First are the financial records. Whether you think of breeding as a hobby or a business, costs accelerate at a sometimes frightening pace.

Unless your resources know no limits, you must at least attempt to break even.

Be realistic. In addition to recording your monthly recurring costs — food, bedding, shampoo, and the like — add vet bills for the year, divided by twelve. Long-term investments — fencing, crates, etc. — should be divided by the months of their life expectancy. If you believe your crates will last five years and they cost sixty dollars each, then the cost is one dollar per month for each crate.

Some months you will have more vet expenses than others, thus warping your averages. In a like manner, some months have more days, which will boost your food expense for that month. Do not get upset. Accuracy to the penny is not what we are after.

To these costs you must add your costs of attending shows, including entry fees, travel expenses, meals, and sometimes overnight expenses. What you are calculating is your advertising expense. The simple fact is that many buyers of show dogs want purebred puppies from parents who have Champion written next to their names. By attending shows and winning, dog people and would-be dog people learn of the existence of your kennel and see your champions in the making. The word spreads. Those interested in your breed start calling. It does not do any good to breed puppies that people don't buy. True, puppy sales are not the reason for breeding. But it is a necessary evil if your breeding program is to continue.

Once you have all your costs and a rough average cost per month, go over your cancelled checks and credit card balances one last time. Are there any hidden costs? What about the facility, the section of the house given to dog use only (the basement, a converted garage, a room in the house)? What about utility and heat costs?

To the year's rent or mortgage charges add a year of utility and heat bills. Now calculate the total area, per floor, of your home and outbuildings and divide that into the cost total. It's really not complicated. Let's use easily managed numbers for an example. Mortgage or rent costs amount to $6,000 per year. Add utilities and heat of $2,400 per year. The monthly average is then $700. To keep it simple, let's say you have a ranch-style house of 2,000 square feet equally divided between first floor and cellar, and no outbuildings. Eighty percent of the house cellar is devoted entirely to dogs. Eight hundred square feet, or forty percent of the house, is for kennel use. Forty percent of $700 per month, or $280, represents the cost of devoting eighty percent of the cellar to dogs. Add this to your monthly costs.

Once you add in these figures, you will have arrived at your total costs per month. If you multiply by twelve you have your total costs per year. Now you must calculate income.

Can You Claim Your Kennel as a Business?

We come to an interesting intersection. If you wish to claim your kennel as a business, the IRS will expect you to seek a profit. Let's say you have settled on having two litters per year and feel reasonably sure you can sell the puppies you do not keep. In your breed, on the average seven pups survive per litter. To increase your breeding stock, you plan to keep one from the first several litters.

Here we will grab some numbers out of the air. Your costs per year come out to $7,000. The price you announce for your pups is $500 each. For fourteen puppies, that makes $7,000. (Whether you sell all the puppies to others or keep two yourself, your kennel income is still $7,000.)

Decision time! If you are trying to make a profit, and have in fact declared that intention to the IRS, a business plan that only breaks even, at best, will not get rave reviews. You could forget to mention some of your expenses and make it look like you made a profit, but then you would find yourself paying taxes on money you did not make. Obviously that is not a sound solution.

You must either increase income or reduce expense. The latter course will be difficult in light of the fact that you are adding to the animal population. There will be more crates, food, shows, vet bills, etc. What then? Raise puppy prices? But others, perhaps more established others, are only asking $500. One other possibility is to have three litters.

We suggest you charge what you have to, regardless of what others charge. Go over every aspect of your costs and cut where you can, if only a dollar at a time. Only if you have a lot of patience and are home much of the time should you consider a third litter.

Breeding Records

Once you have your financial records organized, you should start your breeding records. More exactly, you should continue your breeding records. You started with Throck's pedigree and the stud's pedigree, continued with the breeding data, temperature charts, and descriptions of the babies as they were born. Keep all that information safely filed.

The A.K.C. requires some very specific recordkeeping. That safely filed pedigree information is part of it. Probably the simplest method of complying with their requirements is by using the recordkeeping book they put out, which is called *Dog Ownership and Breeding Records* They enclose an order form with each set of litter registrations. We keep all of our registration certificates attached to their individual record pages. There is space for litter information in the second half of the book. To keep good records is not just a good idea, but should be an ironclad rule. You will need to record who produced what, to whom was it sold, and with what paperwork.

After two weeks from whelping, when you are reasonably sure all the litter still living will survive, register the litter with the A.K.C. We think the instructions given for filling it out are quite clear. Note, however, that more, or different, forms are needed if the breeding resulted from artificial insemination. Those necessary forms are available from the A.K.C. also, at 5580 Centerview Drive, Suite 200, Raleigh NC 27606 - 3390.

So much for the A.K.C. paperwork. But you are not through. Your next step is an evaluation comparing the pups to the breed standard. If the standard mentions head size, measure each puppy's head and record the data. Pasterns are of concern? Measure the length of the pasterns, angle of pasterns, or whatever it is that concerns the breed owners about pasterns. If you do not understand all the language in the standard, pick up the phone and ask one of your fellow breeders. Too, most breed standards are now discussed on videotape with elaborate explanations supported by examples. The tapes are available through the American Kennel Club.

Why all this work? Because you are a breeder now, not just a master of animals. Your aim is to produce dogs that approach the standard or better it. By keeping records of what pairings produce what results, you are better able to assign dominance and use it to your advantage in the future.

In addition to being a breeder, you are also forced to be a vendor. You cannot keep every puppy. The people who buy from you will want you to give them a prediction of what the mature dog will look like, especially if they intend to show the animal. Your kennel reputation may well rise or fall on the accuracy of those predictions.

If, for example, your records show that a pup with a three-inch wide backskull, at three months, will invariably mature to have a head worthy of a Champion, you can assure the puppy buyer and your good reputation will spread. On the dark side, ignore records and guess results. Then watch what happens when you guess wrong.

The point is, you are not breeding dogs just to provide the world with more puppies. The world is teeming with puppies. Your breeding program must have dimension and direction, and be responsible to those who buy its production. Breeding is a science, not a game. Keep accurate records, both paper and photographic. Compare each litter to those records and add their data. You will soon be able to use that information to determine directions that will lead to the realization of goals.

Is having fun and keeping records all there is to raising a litter? Not at all. There is the exhausting ordeal of choosing a registered name for each. The name you bestow will stay with that baby forever, even though the subsequent owner may call the puppy by some other name.

A caution! When the first litter arrives, and even the second, you will assure yourself that you will never forget a single detail of any of those pups, let alone their names. After your tenth litter, unless you are a computer, you will discover your error.

To ease the strain of remembering and associating the pup with the proper parents and bloodlines, theme your litters. We have, for example, litters whose members all have tea names, spice names, country song names, and so on. When a vaguely remembered owner approaches us at a show, writes, or calls in the night, the ability to quickly associate the animal with a theme, and, thereby, its parents and approximate age, certainly saves time and embarrassment.

EARLY TRAINING?

As to early training of the litter, we do little. Some lead break, teach stairs, and all those good fundamentals. We leave those for the new owner who wants to establish himself as the leader of the pack. Our training program is satisfied with teaching those babies to love and be loved.

Please remember that our warning — "If they can, they will" — triples in validity with puppies. Think all the time. Make a mistake and you will pay. They explore; they chew; they reduce mass to the smallest components.

8.

Parting Is Not
Sweet Sorrow

There are breeders who will tell you they cannot wait to get the puppies sold. Probably they mean what they say when they say it. Or they think they do. Then the day comes when that first customer arrives and the puppy goes to a new home.

WHEN TO SELL THE PUPPIES

When that occurs is your choice. There are those who insist that a puppy should leave at seven weeks to assure bonding with his new family. There may well be a sound basis of evidence to support that position. We doubt it.

Our observations over the years lead us to believe that the puppy's ability to bond, at any age, depends on how he is raised to that day. If he and his siblings are handled and loved several times daily by human adults and children, and are allowed to mix with adult dogs in supervised play, those puppies will be prepared to bond with a loving new pack mate at any age.

We keep most of our puppies for at least four months. Why? Because we love them and do not want them to leave, for one thing. The fact that we cannot tell great pet quality from show quality until after the arrival of adult canines at four months plus also plays a part.

The point we wish to make here is that the choice is yours. Do not sell off your puppies too soon because some people try to convince you into believing your puppies will not bond with new people after seven weeks. Raise them properly and there will be no problem. And don't ruin the hard-won reputation of your kennel and your breeding stock by selling as a show grade animal a non-competitive pup.

CHOOSING BUYERS

Some breeders advertise their pups in all-breed magazines, newspapers, and breed publications. Word of mouth through kennel clubs and other breed owners brings new customers. The ranks of people waiting for your pups continue to swell when you and your Champion make an impressive showing in competition. Before you know it, letters and calls will come from all over the country. When the puppies arrive, who should you honor with those lives?

Again, choices abound. You might prefer to see your pups with those who already have a reputation in the breed, who perhaps have political connections with certain judges. Then again, you may only place with the wealthy, those who can supply air-conditioned motor homes, professional handlers, and the like. Or you may want to place them in a geographical region that is most similar to their ancestors' country of origin. Then too — the list goes on and on and on.

The procedure we follow is quite simplistic. When a would-be Clumber owner contacts us, whether at a show, by letter, by telephone, or otherwise, we try our best to provide them with a balanced portrait of a Clumber. With what we hope is equal emphasis, the Clumber's positives and negatives are described. If the inquirer is still interested, we inform him that we breed only ten to fourteen puppies a year, that we have an extensive waiting list, and that purchasers from western Pennsylvania and eastern Ohio automatically jump to the head of the list. (If the puppy owners live close by, we might get to see the animals we bred and their new pack members now and again.) If the person is still interested, we record name and pertinent information. We also issue an invitation to come and see the kennel and the Clumbers.

We never sell a puppy to someone we must ship the puppy to. There could be an exception to that rule if the buyer was well-known to us or it was another dog person whose judgment we trust. But at present, if the buyer cannot at least make one trip to pick up the baby, then another breeder is a better bet for them.

Some are not Right for the Puppy

Practically everyone loves a puppy. Those who would own one, however, are not always as thrilled about what the pup grows into. A couple of examples will elaborate this.

Not long ago, two couples of about the same age, from approximately the same distance away, came to purchase their puppies. Both had been screened by phone and appeared appropriate Clumber owners. Coincidentally, in both instances the pups were to be the birthday presents for wife and mother.

The first couple came to stay the weekend. They brought four children. The parents asked questions about the adults in residence and listened attentively to the elaborate answers. They watched tapes, looked at pictures, and played with adults and puppies, as did the children. Because they wanted a show quality bitch, they also asked for some preliminary handling lessons.

The second couple compared favorably to the first, offering a fenced yard and suburban setting. This couple also brought two children. They did not have time to stay over or assess the puppy's parents and ancestors. Dad gave his attention to the football game. The children chased the cats, not the dogs. Mom did her best to convince us that the puppy's propensity for chewing, shedding, and occasional submissive urinating were expected problems and tolerable.

The reader can probably guess that the second couple made us have severe reservations. Only because they had saved and planned for several months, called several times, and traveled a long distance, did we set aside our doubts and complete the sale.

Two days later, to our immense relief, the little bitch sold to the second couple returned. The woman allowed her two under-ten-year-old children to roughhouse with the puppy. When the excited puppy piddled, the love affair ended and back came the only puppy we have ever had returned.

The point of these examples is to show that you really cannot calculate the merits of a would-be owner until you watch them interact with the animals. A great test is to put them in a room with five or six affectionate adults at a time. The people capable of only lukewarm affection or less stand out immediately. The first couple of our example, by the way, give their puppy a wonderful home.

THE DEPARTURE

Whether your choice of buyer proves fortuitous or questionable, the puppy's departure will hurt. Being certain the baby will have an excellent home makes it easier, but not a lot easier.

Many ask whether the puppy's mother or the puppy's siblings show any sign of missing the baby who leaves. Many experts say no, that the others are programmed by nature to accept such leave-takings. This makes us wonder if the experts ever bred a litter. Our observations lead us to believe that quite the opposite is true. Each time a pack member leaves, the others respond negatively. Quiet prevails. The others lie about in a sort of melancholy state. Sometimes, depending on what happens when to distract them from their sadness, the pack mourns for several hours; other times for days.

We try to get the new owners off to a good start. The buyer is assured that we are at their disposal for help with training and/or showing. The answers to their questions, to the extent that we know them, are always just a phone call away.

The documents that the purchaser carries away include the health record, history, and five generation pedigree. If the pup's sire and dam are in residence, and its grandparents for that matter, we make them available to anyone requesting pictures.

And that's not all! We also throw in a jug of water, a bag of food, and a cloth. By having a jug of our water, the owner can gradually switch the pup to the new water and avoid loose stool. A bag of the food we use and an explanation of why we use it provides the buyer with one direction he can take to assure his animal has proper nutrition. The cloth? It's just any old cloth that has been rubbed over the littermates. Wrapping that cloth around a tick-tock clock and having it in a corner of the puppy's crate can make it possible for both puppy and new people to get more sleep those first few nights.

Do we make our puppy buyers sign a contract? Yes, we do, for what it's worth. Only honorable people adhere to contracts and they are the people you could bind with a shake of the hand. Those who lack honor also break contracts. Will we go to court with our contract? If necessary, you bet. In any event, a copy of our contract is offered below.

Rose Run Kennels   Robert & Toni Freeman
Clumber Spaniels   P.O. Box 345
(412) 465-2439   Penn Runn, PA 15765

Sales Contract

(A) This agreement is made on _____, 19___ between
Robert B. & Toni C. Freeman (the seller)
and _____ (the buyer).

(B) The seller agrees to sell and deliver to the buyer
one _____ Clumber Spaniel
whelped on: _____, 19____
sired by: _____
and out of: _____
AKC Registration #: _____ or AKC Litter # _____ .

(C) The seller also agrees to supply to the buyer a duly completed application for AKC Registration of this Clumber Spaniel.

(D) The seller agrees to sell:

_____ outright

_____ on co-ownership,

and hereby does sell for the purchase price of $_____, a:

_____ show quality

_____ pet quality (AKC registration pending veterinary notification of neutering/spaying).

(E) Said sale is contingent upon the conditions to be performed by the seller and/or buyer as hereinafter set forth:

1. The seller will furnish to the buyer, at time of sale, a five generation pedigree, and a health record of said Clumber Spaniel.

2. The seller considers the dog in sound body and good health, and free from communicable diseases as far as appears to the eye.

3. The buyer recognizes that the Clumber Spaniel breed is subject to the same orthopedic problems that afflict any large, heavy breed, and that these problems do not ordinarily manifest themselves until maturity. The seller does not guarantee any dog against Hip Displasia, Cervical Disc Disease, Elbow Displasia, or any other such condition, nor shall seller be held responsible for same.

4. The buyer agrees that the dog may be used at stud free of charge to the seller on any bitch owned or co-owned by the seller, three times during the life of the dog. If this dog is transferred to a new owner at any time, the stud right mentioned herein must be agreed to in writing by the new owner and by all subsequent owners.

5. The buyer agrees that the bitch, at the time of the first breeding, will be re-registered to include seller as co-owner until such time as the litter is registered, in order to allow seller to be co-breeder of the first litter. Seller will receive second pick of the litter. Seller also will have choice of stud dog for this first litter. When this requirement has been satisfied, all ownership and rights return to the buyer.

6. The buyer agrees and binds himself to take good and reasonable care of the dog, feed and house the dog properly, control the dog on lead when off the premises to avoid loss by theft, running away, or otherwise, and promptly to give or secure the best of attention to the physical and emotional welfare of the dog.

7. The buyer agrees not to change, or alter in any way, the registered name of the dog.

8. The buyer is granted all rights of ownership, or percentage thereof if co-ownership, including whatever income there may be from stud fees or sale of puppies, except as may be specifically provided for in this agreement.

9. If show quality, the buyer agrees to make all reasonable effort to show this dog to its championship and to provide sellers with information as to progress, i.e., shows attended, name of judge and competition, placement. Should the buyers subsequently find showing this dog a problem, the buyer agrees to allow seller to show this dog at major point shows, at buyer's expense.

10. The buyer retains the right to return dog to seller, if for any reason the dog does not meet with his approval within (7) working days following date of purchase. Buyer will incur any shipping costs to return dog.

11. The buyer agrees to notify the seller of any intention to transfer ownership of this dog, or intention to place this dog in the permanent care of another party. The buyer further agrees to grant to the seller in such an event the right of first refusal to purchase the dog at then current fair market value.

12. Additional conditions of sale pertaining to this specific contract:

_____

_____

_____

_____

_____

13. The death or loss or destruction of the dog due to theft, or carelessness, or recklessness will not entitle the buyer to

any compensation, nor does it release the buyer from further payments in the event final payment has not been made. However, in the event of the dog's death from disease or sickness within one year of the date of purchase, if the buyer notifies the seller immediately and furnishes a Veterinary Certificate of Death with full information, the seller may elect to furnish another dog of approximate quality to the buyer at one-half the price of the first dog.

The buyer has this day paid, in full, to the seller the amount of $_____. In so doing the buyer agrees to the terms of this contract.

Seller

Buyer

Thus another breeding cycle is completed. The compassionate buyer will call you now and then, bring the pup to visit, and send a picture in the Christmas card. In actuality, quite a few do that the first year, not so many the second year, and practically none after that.

The breeders? Those who chose to continue — the good ones — will take time to evaluate the experience, recognize mistakes, search for better ways, and underline victories. After a few weeks for the wounds to begin healing, the breeders will be matchmaking again. This time they may experience a major tragedy—the loss of Mom or a litter. Such events tend to reduce the number of breeders. Still, some breeders persist. They see it all, they suffer it all, yet their dedication to the breed forces them into the fray. They breed until the bucket fills and there is not more room for pain. Then they teach others.

9.

The Geriatrics

Before we leave the subject of breeding, we must discuss the most often overlooked component, or by-product, of that endeavor — the geriatrics.

KEEPING DOGS BEYOND BREEDING AGE

Would-be breeders must make provisions in their plans for those animals who no longer contribute to the program or who may be temporarily on the shelf. We ask for only two litters from each of our bitches, at ages two and four, or at three and five. They are then spayed to prolong their lives and health.

If you keep one or more males, and you eventually will, remember that you can use him at stud only sparingly. Breed him to a bitch, then wait a minimum of four years before you bring him back to a grandchild.

The whole picture paints well. Breeders are surrounded by wonderful dogs they love. The shadows thicken, however, when you study the practical aspects. The geriatrics keep eating. They also keep needing exercise, personal attention, and more than their share of vet visits. That is all not to mention crates and a place to spend the day. All this time the young require like equipment and supplies and add their excrement to the scooper's task.

What to do? Plan carefully! Calculate the number of animals your program will require. Now factor out those numbers in terms of money, time, and facility capacity. Stay conservative.

Some breeders sell their older animals as soon as the time arrives that the animal no longer contributes. We do not oppose that plan. We even tried it — once. There was too much pain involved. The animal who has daily shared your life for four to seven years does not sell easily. So we keep ours now.

HEALTH PROBLEMS

The older animals, like older people, can have a variety of ailments. That is because older people and older animals have one very insidious thing in common — they are both dying.

It is not as easy to see old age in a dog as it is in a human. At least it is more difficult than assessing the age of people who have not altered their parts or tucked up against old age.

One of the first things you will notice is that the geriatric becomes less active. Not that she is without energy or refuses commands. That is not the case. We have a bitch, Tina, who, after two litters, came out of conformation retirement and finished her CD at nine or so. No, it's just that they moderate both the quantity and exuberance of their responses to life around them.

If the animal does show a growing reluctance to respond immediately, it may well be another by-product of age — deafness. As with people, with age dogs often go deaf, blind, or both. They can lose teeth and suffer arthritis. None of these maladies is life-threatening, but any or all can cause more work for the breeder.

Also in common with the elderly humans is the geriatric dog's capacity to handle temperature extremes, both hot and cold. Restrict outside time to mornings and evenings during the summer; bright and midday hours during the winter. Geriatrics of both human and dog origin resist sudden changes in routine. Softly and easily is a better approach than abruptly and insistently.

TAKING CARE OF OLDER DOGS

Can we do anything to ease our animal through the geriatric period? Yes! Will it require more time and expense? Yes and yes!

Check eyes, ears, and teeth daily. Keep them clean. Feed a dry kibble and lower the protein to eighteen percent, give or take a little, with reduced salt. An inactive geriatric cannot use the amount of protein intended for an animal working the field. Excess proteins cause deposits in the kidneys and can speed up failure of those vital organs. Obesity is as harmful to a dog as it is to a human. Cut food quantity and increase supervised activity to keep the geriatric slim and trim.

No matter what precautions are taken, the owner and the geriatric will not escape death. Ultimately death will visit both and come away victorious.

It is a terribly sad time!

Too often owners assume that death will visit the pet first. Too often the owner is wrong. The owner usually provides for human family members, but what of the companion who has unconditionally loved and accepted love for all its life?

If you took the time to draw up a will, then take the time to prepare a codicil appointing a guardian for the animal. Include a sum of money from your estate to maintain the animal. (If there is any chance the will may be contested, warn your attorney and have him establish a trust.)

Dogs mourn also! If at all possible, arrange with the guardian to allow the animal to sleep with an article of the owner's clothing, even to visit the grave occasionally.

DEATH

When the animal goes first, be certain you are ready. That is actually poor advice, because you can never be ready. But fool yourself by thinking through the possibilities and planning action in advance.

The worst scenario is when you take your ailing friend to the vet and get only a negative shake of the head. Life could be prolonged, but not without continued pain and even further loss of capacity. The alternative is euthanasia.

We wish that we knew a way to make this decision easier for you. But there is nothing easy about it. To pick up a trusting friend in your arms and carry it to swift but certain death will rip out your heart. The assurance that you are showing your friend a merciful way out does little to ease the agony of the survivor.

There is also the question of what to do with the remains. Many people, somehow, leave disposal to the vet and walk away. As a rule, the vet then sends the remains to the incinerator in a plastic bag. For a fee, there are incinerators that selectively cremate. They will return the ashes to you and assure you they are your animal's. Ashes require only a small grave. Land owners have the option of claiming the remains and burying. (Though you should check to see if there is an ordinance against it in your area.) Although there is pain in the digging, there is also therapy. The digging provides an opportunity for open grief. Use the opportunity and purge your heart.

And how do you handle the next day? Again we wish we knew a perfect answer. We do not.

Do animals go to heaven? Through history, several groups, from Egyptians to American Indians, have assigned them a place in the hereafter. Examine your faith and make a decision you can live with.

Probably the most comforting possibility is to have another dog, a younger model to turn to. Each animal has its own personality and no two are the same, but the love and understanding will be close.

II

THE BIG TIME

10.

Reach for the Stars

We are happy to report that Throckmortana's pregnancy went smoothly, as did the whelping. There was one stillborn puppy, which occasioned tears, but no problems for bitch or litter beyond that. (Authoring is much easier than breeding. The story always comes out the way we want it to in this book.)

Let's say that Lynnedora and Throck raised the puppies carefully and four of seven went to pet homes. Two show quality puppies got snapped up quickly. Lynnedora and family kept the pick bitch. They intend to continue breeding.

But now Lynnedora has reached an impasse. A new season of dog shows has started; the family, including Lynnedora, looks forward to participating.

We certainly agree that they should, if they have anything to compete. The puppy is, of course, too young. The boy we loaned them will not be competitive for another year. He's out of an English import and a line that matures very slowly.

"What about Throck?" Lynnedora asks. "She has recovered wonderfully and moves at least as well as she ever did. Every time she hears the wagon start, she heads to the door with tail wagging. She misses the show ring."

A year—the time it would take for either the loaned boy or the new girl to get competitive — is a long time for the family to drop out. We understand Lynnedora's position. Equipment wanders, impatient children develop other interests. The sport allowed family and animal to do something as a team and she does not want to chance losing the enthusiasm and momentum.

We certainly agree. They have been good for the sport and the sport has been good for them. On the other hand, following a new path that leads to defeat after defeat will do little to assure their long-range participation. They just embarked on a breeding program. What a disaster it would be if the family takes Throck into a level where she is not competitive, and, as a result, loses their confidence in all they could accomplish.

CHOOSING TO PURSUE A SPECIALTY

What are their choices? There are several, really: Group Ring and Best-in-Show, of course; Campaigning a special; Challenging the International set; National specialties; Westminster! How far they can go, or if they should go at all, depends on Throck. To attempt any or all of these challenges, the animal must be exceptional. Is Throck exceptional?

Many are deluded into believing their animal is exceptional because it is entitled to use the word Champion before its name. This is the first error. Sometimes that word means less than others. The cruel fact is that all too often very average, even poor, representatives of a breed win an A.K.C. Championship. If the animal's owner sticks with it long enough, enters the animal in enough shows under enough judges, sooner or later the animal will finish. This may not be true always, but it is very, very often.

Kennel Blindness

This is unfortunate! We use that word advisedly. Seeing that word Champion before their animal's name often leads to a serious malady for breeders known in the sport as "kennel blindness." It is a serious malady, seldom if ever entirely cured. The malady causes an owner to hallucinate.

You think we are teasing. Well, we may be, a little. But only a little. Owners with kennel blindness pretend to give an honest evaluation of their animal in terms of the breed standard. They are quite serious in their approach. But their eyes and hands betray them. They assess an animal that is far better than their own, with assets their Champion will never possess.

Do not question their evaluation or challenge their results. No amount of dissenting opinion dissuades them. They see what they want to see and that is the end of it. They are convinced their animal is a late bloomer and ready to take on the world. It will be a rude awakening when the owner realizes he and his animal have challenged in an arena where they are not competitive. The lesson can be very expensively learned.

We sympathize with these people. Their disappointment could be avoided if judges were required to be more informative when choosing their winners. As it stands now, entrants pay for an evaluation and get only "one, two, three," from the judge. If the A.K.C. would require their judges to accompany their placement with an educated and meaningful written evaluation, owners of marginal dogs would not be deluded.

Lynnedora must avoid kennel blindness. Before she and the family seriously consider taking Throck to Group or dueling with the International set, they must put aside the prejudices that grow from their love of Throck. For just a few moments they must view her objectively and honestly evaluate their girl for type, movement, and attitude.

CONDITIONS OF SPECIALTY SHOWING

In Throck's case, she is going to have to be better than top-notch. There are some truths about the new level of competition that Lynnedora and family must know from the very start.

Bitches are at a Disadvantage

They must keep in mind, for example, that Throck is a bitch. Like it or not, a bitch is usually disadvantaged against a male. At the new level of competition, where the boys are older and flashier than in breed competition, the disadvantage increases. Does that mean that bitches never win the big ones? Most decidedly not. Bitches have won some notable victories. The thing to note is that a good part of what made those victories notable was the fact that a bitch defeated a male.

Professional Handlers Have an Edge

Lynnedora, who, with our applause, insists upon handling her own dog, will find herself in the ring with an abundance of professional handlers as early as the Group level. She might at times find that she is the only non-professional owner-handler in the ring. Is this a disadvantage? In theory, no. We would feel less than honest, however, if we tried to pretend that theory prevails. Though there are judges who are not influenced by handlers, or at least appear to be above such influence, there are many who are touched by that influence. Let's look at that situation a little more closely.

Judges are only human. Most of them come from the ranks of the breeders and/or professional handlers. They thus start their career as judges knowing who the professionals are. Many are their friends. Over the years they read the dog magazines and weekly dog newspapers and see the professionals and their charges in full-page ads. For a judge to enter a ring and pretend non-recognition would be ludicrous.

If recognition were the only by-product, there would be little to fear. But the plot thickens. The judges also know that the professionals need to win often to make a decent living. It is reasonable for the judge to assume, therefore, that a professional will not enter a ring without an animal that is far above average. Whereas the amateur's dog needs to excel to be in contention, the pro's animal, quality or not, must fall on its face to be out of contention.

All this is a great disadvantage to the amateur at this point, but it is not an insurmountable challenge if it stops there. It does not. Judges rely on the various kennel clubs to give them work each weekend. Though the payments will hardly make them wealthy, invitations from the clubs provide them with free travel, social intercourse, and a decent supplement to other income. Unfortunately, professional handlers often influence the clubs' choices of judges. We have heard professionals threaten judges that they will never again receive an assignment in the area. Can the professionals make good on such threats? Unhappily, yes. Kennel clubs' profits depend on the number of entries at their shows. If a professional handler brings twelve entries to any given show, a club would definitely notice his or her absence next year. Until the A.K.C. takes control, assigns judges to shows, and requires them to write a critique on each animal judged, the situation will not be remedied and professionals will win more than their share.

Enough said on that subject to make the point. Professional handlers can be defeated in the Group competition, but it is not easy.

Rare Breeds are at a Disadvantage

Would that Lynnedora's problems ended there. They do not. She must also understand that Throck is a Clumber Spaniel, a rare breed, and that is a distinct disadvantage. An explanation is due. Again walk in the shoes of the judge. The judge knows that often a rare breed makes it to Group because there was no competition in the Breed ring. This does not always happen, certainly, but often it does. The judge also knows that a Cocker Spaniel, for example, probably beat several of its breed to get to Group. That should not matter. Each animal should be evaluated on its own merits. It usually does not happen that way. Far too regularly the rare breed is discounted from the very beginning.

These problems are not presented to discourage Lynnedora. We do believe, however, that she should keep in mind the mountains to be climbed as she stands back and evaluates Throck's chances.

EVALUATING YOUR DOG

The first thing Lynnedora should do as she starts her evaluation is to go to her bookshelf and pull out her copy of the breed standard. While showing our animals to their championships, it is not unusual to blur the words of the standard and think of our animals as the perfect specimen. Once the championship is earned, the words blur even more. As we mentioned, only discipline can prevent the malady of kennel blindness.

Word by word, inch by inch, Lynnedora must apply the A.K.C. standard for the breed to Throck. She has performed this exercise before. It should be easier this time. Lynnedora now has the advantage of having seen all the Clumbers who competed against Throck. Each of those animals was a living interpretation of that very same standard, with variations on the theme.

Gloss over the sections dealing with type for now. We will say more on the subject of type later. Though type should be important in the Group ring, as it is in the Breed ring, it is not. The buzzwords in the Group ring do not include type. The buzzwords are only two — movement and attitude.

MOVEMENT

Lynnedora must appraise these areas one at a time. The standard will help her judge structure — Throck's structure — in terms of breed correctness. A sound structure is the prerequisite for good movement.

If Throck's structure appears to coincide with the standard, it is next for Lynnedora to evaluate Throck's utilization of that structure. Movement is buzzword number one.

Do not be misled. Assessing movement is anything but easy. Neither is it easy to reduce to words what Lynnedora and the reader should look for. Movement is an area wherein verbal descriptions give way to the wordless perceptions of the experienced eye.

Let's start by warning Lynnedora that a handler can do very little to help a dog who moves well to move better. But the handler can do much to ruin the movement of a good moving dog. The animal shown on taut lead, for example, with head strung high, should be automatically dismissed from consideration by the judge.

Why are we so harsh? Because an animal that is strung up cannot move correctly. To move properly, a dog must have the freedom to lunge with his head, enhancing his body's forward thrust. The rear legs supply the power, a strong and firm back carries the mass of the body forward, the neck and head continue the thrust, and the forelegs catch and lift the weight into position for a repeat of the sequence.

The great movers accomplish all of this motion with economy and seemingly little expenditure of effort. Each foot falls in perfect rhythm and moves on again without the slightest interference with the other feet.

Lynnedora and our readers would be well advised to attend a show, or several, without animal. Relax for an afternoon and watch every dog move that you can. Do not try to reduce everything you see to words. You trust your eyes with the beauty of a sunset. Trust them also with the beauty of a good animal in motion.

The current fad among self-appointed movement experts is to claim the ability to assess a dog's movement by watching the side movement only. This is an exciting proposal doomed to fail. Viewing a dog in motion from the side can tell the observer several things about the animal's movement, but it cannot reveal everything about the animal's movement.

What should Lynnedora watch for?

She should look for balance, or nothing in excess. Start by watching side movement as the judges do. While the animal courses the ring, the head should drop slightly each time the neck and body thrust.

The feet should fall with perfect rhythm. The back should remain strong and firm. The front legs should reach far enough to pull the body forward, but not so far that they have no ability to lift. The rear legs must supply thrust, but not so much that the animal falls over its front feet. All must be coordinated to allow the animal to cover the ground without expending needless energy. The animal should be able to continue for long periods of time.

Watch closely as the handler moves the animal in a direct line away from you. If the dog's rear appears to shift sidewards even as it moves forward, you are watching a dog that is crabbing. Imagine him following a line across a football field. If his body appeared to move across, but with the body always on a diagonal to the line rather than straight with the line, we have crabbing. Crabbing occurs when the rear assembly is too strong for the front or when the rear feet are too far reaching. To avoid having his rear feet collide with his front feet, he angles them to the side.

Let's assume you saw no crabbing. The rear assembly remained straight with the imaginary line; the rear legs powered the animal forward in a rhythmic fashion. You see what the judge sees. It may not be the best rear in the animal kingdom, but there is nothing apparent to fault.

Imagine that line across the football field again. The handler turns his animal and starts toward you. Wait, your mind says. Did that animal flick out its foot during the turn and appear for a tiny moment to lose its command of the ground? In the sport that fault is called "puppy hocks." What it means is that the animal has loose joints at the ankle. When he turns, much like children on ice skates, the ankle refuses to support the body. Be alert as you watch. The fault is there and gone in a second.

You are now down the home stretch. Watch the elbows. Are they held close in to the body, or do they bow as the animal moves? Do the front feet hold a line, or do they break out away from the line? You think they paddle, as it is called. Keep watching that front. Does it appear as though the front is doing the job of pulling the animal forward? It does. Now comes the critical part. Does the front appear to lift the body after each thrust and prepare it for a new power sequence? We realize it's all happening very quickly. Concentrate and study. There is no apparent lift. Then your original assessment is probably correct; the animal is paddling.

Lynnedora will undoubtedly miss many things her first time out. Unless a person has spent a lifetime around animals, most do miss a lot the first time out, and the second, fifth, and even twentieth. If judging were easy, everyone would be doing it.

At this stage, Lynnedora can only make the attempt and keep practicing. She should try to mingle with the veterans at ringside and listen to their comments. A warning needs to be given here. Veteran status does not necessarily imply a good eye for movement. Sort and sift and accept nothing as the absolute truth.

A real assist is the video recorder. Go to a quality show and film the group competition. Study the film in the comfort of your TV room as often as you wish. If you have slow motion, by all means use it. Have one of the family film you and Throck. Compare it to the group competition. If you truly believe, as Lynnedora does, that your Throck has no obvious motion deficiencies, so much for the first buzzword.

ATTITUDE

We said earlier that there are two buzzwords when it comes to Group competition—movement and attitude. For the latter word you may hear some people substitute showmanship. Since we believe showmanship is the by-product of attitude, we will keep with the former.

Only the animal's handler can truthfully evaluate its attitude. The road ahead is demanding of people and the animal. Does Throck truly love going to shows, or does she just love pleasing the family that wants her to go to shows? There will be long hours of travel, confinement, and irregular routine. Can Throck handle that and still burst into the ring, tail on wag, ready to compete?

Far too often we witness situations in which we discover it is the owner who enjoys the shows, the travel, and the competition. The animal's tail still wags, but out of dedication, not enthusiasm. Owners of Champions are not always champion people. At the expense of their animal, they continue making entries. Their egos feed on the glory that emanates from their animals' victories, yet they will be quick to list the many sacrifices they have made on behalf of the dog. Why else would they go through the ordeal, week after week, if not for the animal?

Movement and attitude. If you are sure Throck is solid in both areas, the Group ring awaits. It is the gateway to the major league. Have at it. And succeeding there, there are other mountains to climb. We will consider them all, but give one word of caution first. Watch Throck and the family carefully. If the ordeal proves too taxing, the tail stops wagging, and the smiles disappear, go home. It's only a game. Breeding is life and death. The sport of showing is only a game.

11.

Group and Best-in-Show

Some of our readers did not share with us Lynnedora's and Throck's climb to a Championship. For them, and as a review for the many rookies in the sport, we would like to take the time here to review the Breed Ring format, which is the level we, with tongue in cheek, refer to as the sport's minor league.

THE BREED RING FORMAT

It is important that the reader understand this sequence because there is no open invitation to Group. Champion or not, each time out your animal must prevail at Breed level to gain access to Group. It works as follows.

When the time arrives for your breed to be judged, the steward of the designated ring will call out the numbers assigned by the show Superintendent to the youngest males registered. In the ideal situation having a large entry with all classes represented, the first class called by the steward would be the Puppy Dogs — 6 to 9 months. Once the winner of that class is decided, the call goes out in succession for Puppy Dogs — 9 to 12 months, American Bred Dogs, Bred-by-Exhibitor Dogs, and Open Dogs.

At the end of the sequence, the winners of each class return to compete against one another. In theory at least, the judge will decide whether the younger dogs are better examples of young dogs of the breed than the older dogs are examples of older dogs of the breed, or vice versa. The dog that prevails is awarded the purple ribbon.

It's not over. The Winner's Dog retires from the ring and is replaced by the dog who went second to him in the class competition. (If it happens that he was the only one entered in that class, the competition continues among the other class winners.) The award this time is the purple and white Reserve Winner's ribbon. Should the Winner's Dog later be disqualified, the Purple ribbon passes to the Reserve Winner.

Now come the Bitches, called in the same order as are the dogs. Winner's Bitch and Reserve Winner's Bitch ribbons are awarded. The steward next announces the Best-of-Breed competition. If novices manage to keep things straight through reserve, they usually crumble to confusion here. It is not all that complicated.

Where people get lost is in recognizing that there are really two competitions that take place in the next segment. The steward calls into the ring the Winner's Dog, the Winner's Bitch, and all challengers who are already A.K.C. Champions.

Follow this next part carefully. Let us assume we are watching Throckmortana returned to her days in the Open Class, those days before she became a Champion. Going in, she needs five points and a major to finish. Each Winner is entitled to the points available to its sex that particular day, up to a maximum of five points. (Points depend on the number of animals present.) We will say, for instance, that the Irving Dog won three points and a major because of the number of dogs present. Poor Throckmortana won only two points and no major for her victory. But it's not over yet.

The sub-competition and first to be decided by the judge is the competition between Irving and Throckmortana. Assume that Throckmortana wins in the judge's mind. She will receive nothing until this segment is concluded, but with the judge's decision she is now entitled to the blue-and-white ribbon awarded to Best-of-Winners, and more. Irving loses none of his points, but Throckmortana deserves the same number of points that Irving takes home. She did beat him. When she gets the ribbon, she also gets a three point major.

Now the judge compares Best-of-Winners and the Champions. This is all going on in his mind. He does not yet announce Best-of-Winners or send any of the animals from the ring. Although he has chosen the Best-of-Winners in his mind, he can still change that decision.

Assume again that Throckmortana not only claims Best-of-Winners, she also defeats two male Champions and a female Champion for Best-of-Breed. If the two males are added to the other males present and that total involves another point or two, she can win five points, including a major, Best-of-Winners, and Best-of-Breed. One of the other dogs in the Best-of-Breed competition will be awarded Best-of-Opposite Sex to her.

By taking Best-of-Breed, Throckmortana wins one very important additional laurel — an invitation to compete in the Group Competition, the first plateau of what we call the major league of the sport.

Pitfalls of a Rare Breed

This is all well and good, but recall our earlier warnings to Lynnedora. She will be competing a young bitch against mature males and, worse, a bitch that represents a rare breed.

To elaborate on why that is a problem, let us provide you with another scenario. Throck shows up at Breed Ring to find that no other Clumbers are entered. The competition and evaluation will proceed, but it is only Throck against the standard. A Best-of-Breed win is not assured, nor is a Group invitation. The judge could decide that Throck is not a good representative of the breed and should not be reproduced. He could award her a second place ribbon and deprive her of her invitation. Such things do happen and probably should happen more often. Sad to say that when it does happen now, the withholding judge is usually just trying to make a name.

If the judge, however, awards her Best-of-Breed, an almost certain outcome with a Champion involved, competition or no, Throck is entitled to compete in Group. Now we get to the point of this diversion. The Group judge can safely believe that popular breed representatives have defeated some numbers of their breed to get there and, thus, at least in the Breed judge's opinion, are worthy specimens. But what of the rare breed entrant? Was there a strong field, or did she triumph by default; is she a good specimen, or only just above marginal? Too often the judge, not really comfortable with the breed, will assume the worst.

GROUP COMPETITIONS

"Well this time we earned our ticket," reminds Lynnedora. "Throck took down three Specials. What we need to know now is what exactly are we getting into by accepting that Group invitation?"

It is just more animals and more people in a somewhat larger ring. That might be understating things slightly, but the last thing we want to do is to build up the competition to more than it is and leave the handler feeling intimidated. A nervous handler transmits that lack of confidence down the lead to the animal. A case of the jitters can defeat animal and handler before the competition starts.

Let's start from the beginning. The Group competitions follow the Breed competitions. The partitions are removed from between two or more Breed rings to create one large ring. You will recognize it immediately upon seeing the large wooden numbers, 1 through 4, in the center of the ring. The numbers are there for a purpose. Four places are awarded in each competition.

How many competitions are there? Seven — Sporting, Non-Sporting, Working, Hound, Toy, Herding, and Terrier. (The breeds included in each group are listed in the appendix.) The order in which the Groups will compete on a given day is listed in both the judging program and the catalog for that show. Do not count on these lists entirely. If one of the breeds of a group is still being judged at the time that Group is due in the ring, the order can change. Don't worry, though. The need for change is usually determined well enough in advance to allow the loudspeakers to announce the change. Stay alert. The announcement may require you to shift gears quickly.

Throckmortana, a Clumber Spaniel, must compete in the Sporting Group. We dislike overusing the same phrase, but again we must use those words "in theory." In theory, the judge will assess the animal in terms of its Breed standard. If Throck, then, proves to be a better Clumber than Adolph the Shorthair is a good Shorthair, Throck wins. In theory, at least, that's the way it works.

It is our opinion that reality will never prove theory. A judge would have to have a mind with slots for floppy disks to recall that many standards in such a short time, let alone evaluate and compare all the Group ring animals in terms of their standards. We see it as an impossible task and accept it as such.

In fact, rather than theory, at best most judges reduce the competition to a movement and attitude contest. At worst it is a "who is on the upper end of the lead" contest.

PREPARING FOR THE COMPETITION

How does Lynnedora prepare? She already completed the difficult part when she and Throck practiced being a team on the move. Walk Throck into her favorite gait and then go along for the trip, with the lead flopping. Some handlers lag a little behind the animal to make it look like the animal is a fast moving cloud.

It is always important to stop your animal an appropriate distance from the judge so that the animal can respond alertly to bait or a signal and display expression. In Group it becomes even more important.

Throughout *The Road to Westminster* we preached teamwork between handler and animal. Look around as you enter the Group ring and you will understand the importance of teamwork. Many, if not most, of the animals will be seasoned campaigners, three to six years old, with perhaps hundreds of shows to their credit. You will also notice that on the other end of the lead, with few exceptions, stands a professional handler, also seasoned and with hundreds of shows to the handler's credit. Watch animal and human. You will see teamwork.

Many ringside viewers will insist that only professional handlers ever win Groups. Many, many believe that story. Watch, if you will, the owners whose animals surprise them and take Breed. They can often be seen scouring the grounds for a professional who is without a Group entrant. The first they find who will agree to take their animal into Group is hired.

Why do they do that, you might ask. Now that's somewhat hard to say. Perhaps it is lack of confidence in their own handling ability. They cannot expect the newly-found professional and animal to exhibit any high degree of teamwork. Most likely, they believe those who suspect politics are being played. Certainly the professional they hire will say nothing to allay the suspicion that not all is on the up and up. True or not, the suspicion put fifty or more extra dollars in his pocket.

The truth is that it is difficult to defeat the pros and their charges, but it is not impossible. Both ends of the professional's lead are quality — well-practiced, highly polished quality. But it is not unbeatable quality. In the absence of politics, Lynnedora and Throck stand a chance. What more can they expect than a chance?

Soon Lynnedora will hear someone announce that all dogs eligible for the Sporting Group should stand by outside the Group ring. Well before she hears those words, she should have completed a touch-up of Throck's grooming and have her ready. There should be no mad dashes to the ring to make it in the nick of time. Lynnedora and Throck, in keeping with the other Group contestants, are a class act. Stress has no place in a game designed for fun.

As she leisurely walks to the ring, her attention should be on Throck; not on human friends and not on strangers interested in the breed. There will be time for that after the competition.

Lynnedora should talk to Throck, play with her, assure her they are going to have fun. Together and in concert, they need to get on the jazz. Lynnedora should comb Throck, hug her, tantalize her with a small piece of bait. When Throck walks into that ring, she should demand a ribbon. The handlers who trudge into the ring, leading an animal with tail down and attention wandering, make a serious mistake. Once the game begins, it is too late for the pep talk.

IN THE RING

Once through the gate, the novice will experience a serious and often unpleasant piece of business. Most — almost all — judges are reluctant to assert themselves until after the contestants and their handlers arrange themselves in some semblance of order. As a result, the experienced handlers insist on their favorite positions relative to other handlers and animals, treating those who would presume to trespass with treatment ranging from rudeness to open hostility. The judge should arrange the order in terms of size and ability to cover ground at a natural gait. That almost never happens.

Until experience teaches Lynnedora where Throck is at best advantage, she will often allow the other handlers to disadvantage Throck. She will find herself stacking Throck in a dip or behind a post, dashing to keep up with larger animals, or tagging behind smaller and slower animals.

Round One: Around the Ring

Once the handlers snarl and jostle themselves and their animals into line, most of the judges signal for the handlers to take their dogs around. Then begins a sprint in which animals and people race around the ring at top speed in an attempt to convince the judge that the animal's ability to hold its place in line equates with sound structure and correct movement.

This is the perfect opportunity for Lynnedora to reduce her disadvantage. If she tries to make Throck stay with the setters, she will run her Clumber's legs off. Almost as poor a move is to allow slower animals to break Throck's gait.

What Lynnedora should do to avoid such a disastrous trap is to ignore the rest and move Throck to best advantage. Many judges put great stock in their observations of side gait. Most at least start their elimination process at this stage. If those in front of her wish to dash off, she should let them. There is no rule that requires her to match strides with the rest. She is entitled to move her animal at its proper gait as well as any other handler in the ring.

When those in front dash, she should let the space between them grow and keep Throck at her best. Is there slow traffic ahead? Pass on the inside, always in view of the judge. Should something happen to interrupt Throck's movement, correct her and get her back on gait as quickly as possible. Never, never let her continue with a broken gait or pacing. One never knows. The moment she goes out of gait could be the very moment the judge turns to evaluate Throck.

Round Two: Stacking

Round two varies with the different judges. One thing is sure, it will start immediately after round one. Lynnedora must be ready; she is in fast company. At this level of competition judges have little tolerance for misbehaving animals and inattentive or inept handlers.

That is not to say that both handler and animal cannot be animated and obviously having fun. Though some believe the world stops revolving and awaits the results of such contests, it really is only a game. Keep reminding yourself of that — only a game.

Some judges start the second round by viewing the animals assembled in stack position and examine each in turn. They then move to round three, during which they have the animals moved out and back or in similar patterns. Other judges prefer to combine the two rounds. The judge will call out each animal individually, examine it, and have it moved. When Lynnedora gets home, she should make an entry in her judges' notebook. In the notebook, each judge she shows to should be listed alphabetically, with appropriate comments. Next time she shows to that judge, she will not have to guess what the judge expects in terms of format and patterns.

From the time you finish round one until the competition ends, keep Throck in a natural stack at least. It is easy from that position to adjust Throck into any position required of her.

And there is another reason. At any given moment, whether evaluating Throck or ten animals down the line, the judge may look toward Throck by way of comparison. Do not be shy about assuring that the judge sees Throck at her best. If the judge is looking, Throck is most likely in contention. Stroke her best features to remind the judge. Ask for the victory.

In *The Road to Westminster* we discussed stacking at length. Surely those of you considering the fast lane have long since mastered that art. Your animal's Championship indicates that. The judge wants to see the pleasing profile of a well-balanced animal. Remember, the judge does not want to wait while you fumble the animal into position.

The judge's hands-on examination will be cursory, at best. It is a formality, nothing more, especially if your animal is not one of those that aroused the judge's interest during the first round.

Round Three: Patterning

Moving out and back is another matter. What the judge should be looking for in this pattern, or any other suggested, are the faults we mentioned in the movement section — paddling, crabbing, etc.

We want to see Lynnedora walk Throck into her proper gait, which Throck could maintain all day in the field, then move smoothly in a straight line with her animal. If Throck is one that requires the handler to run to keep up, then Lynnedora should use long strides with her feet landing flat. Choppy, mincing, or bouncy movement by the handler distracts from the smooth flow of the animal's movement.

Should Throck break stride, correct it immediately. The need to correct will not win points, but it is a far better strategy than allowing the animal to proceed until it corrects itself, if it corrects itself. This is the animal's best moment, one on one with the judge. It is a brief moment! Do not waste it.

Round Four: Judge's Inspection

Catch up to your animal's head as you near the judge and bring your animal to a stop a good three to four feet before you reach the judge. At all costs do not let the animal either trample or jump up on the judge. As soon as the animal stops, Lynnedora should claim Throck's attention. Use bait, baby talk, or whatever it takes. Get Throck to show her alertness. A wagging tail will not hurt your animal's presentation.

If the judge wants to try for Throck's attention, by all means concede. Some judges rattle keys, whistle, or snap their fingers. Whatever they try, do not contest the effort. Step aside and hope that Throck favors the judge with an alert response.

Before directing you to a last circuit of the ring, the judge may want one more look at Throck in a natural stack. Have Throck trained to stack herself immediately. So often the handler and animal wind up doing a dance while the judge circles in a vain attempt to catch a glimpse of the animal. Such behavior does not suggest the well-seasoned team that demands the win.

Once around, the judge orders. Easy does it. Unless you are already among the eliminated-from-consideration, the judge wants to concentrate on the fall of Throck's feet. Let Throck move comfortably and do not relax until you are back with the other contestants. When an animal quits early, it suggests that it lacks either the physical attributes or the heart to go the whole way. During hot afternoons at the end of a long weekend, fatigue does start to take a toll. If you think your animal is in trouble, excuse yourself and get to the show vet. If he must travel to get to you, or vice versa, follow the first aid instructions presented in *The Road to Westminster*.

Lynnedora, too, could play out and falter. If she starts to sag, she should go home. It is only a game. That is not to say that she does not owe it to herself, the animal, and the sport to be in condition. Both handler and animal should be toned and fit. On any given day, however, even the best can crumble.

After that individual performance, Throck and handler must wait for the others to have their moment. While we are waiting, let's take a moment to summarize. The way we count, Throck has had four opportunities to impress the judge.

A Summary of the Ring

Round one found her circling the ring. It can be a vicious time, especially if we include the initial assembling. If there are handlers who will resort to dirty tricks to win (and there are many), this is a time to watch for them. From allowing their larger animal to snarl at your smaller animal to dropping bait to running up Throck's back to stepping on Throck's toes, these handlers will attempt anything to gain any little edge they can get. Be wary. When their actions become oppressive, unobtrusively give back better than you take. Next time they will pick on somebody else. (Some consider dirty tricks a left-handed compliment to their animal and themselves. If the others were not concerned about the challenge, they would not bother. Keep in mind, too, that professionals making their living from the sport often lose perspective and forget that the competition is only a game.)

Round two found Throck being subjected to a hands-on inspection. There is nothing much anyone can do to interfere with Throck here. Realistically, the judge can tell very little from such an inspection. A bad mouth, entropion, a fat pad, one testicle — these are a few things that can be picked up here. Muscle impresses the judges. Fat and growls eliminate the animal from contention.

The third round was out and back or some other similar pattern. It is a time for Throck to shine since there are no obstructions other than the terrain and the crowd. Well-practiced at home and earlier shows in the art of traveling a straight line, this is the time that Throck can take group under a judge with a good eye. Of course, in that company, there are probably another half dozen animals who can do the same.

Perhaps the most important round is the fourth. It is the round in which most amateurs do poorly and the round in which most animals are eliminated, whether the judge realizes it or not. The round we speak of has two parts — the test for expression and the natural stack for inspection. To this point, Throck has made a clinical impression. This is her moment of intimacy with the judge; her moment to win the judge's admiration and heart.

Now there is one last time around the ring. Hopefully Throck will show her staying power here and put down and pick up her feet without missing a beat. She will radiate arrogance and keep that tail wagging.

DIRTY TRICKS

This is the time when the owner-handler could easily be bounced from the competition, a victim of "dirty tricks."

What does the handler need to watch for? Some professionals work in teams, even groups. Lynnedora could find herself and Throck squeezed between the animals of non-contenders, front and back. They want Lynnedora to rattle and stack Throck without stretching her out, thus making her back appear roached rather than strong and straight. Further, they hope the close proximity of their animals will distract Throck's attention.

Or handlers may force Lynnedora into a depression in the ground. Stacking Throck there will raise questions about her topline. A handler's foot can "accidentally" crunch toes. Bait drops close to Throck's nose. A popular move is for a professional handler to set up his animal out closer to the judge on an angle calculated to inhibit the judge's view of Throck.

There are more tricks. They appear as fast or even faster than you can devise remedies to combat them. Next show they will change again. The best advice we can offer is to know your job, know your rights, and stay alert. Lynnedora and Throck must perform to the level of the competition. If Throck and Lynnedora act like amateurs, they will certainly be treated accordingly. Whether pro or amateur, there are rules of the game. Learn them and use them. Do not let the competitors intimidate you. Once they do, you will never see the end of it. Wait your turn and zing back. Once you can give as well as take, the harassment will dwindle.

If they gang up and you are not a fighter, you have three choices. Lose; Go home; Stop the contest and enlist the aid of the A.K.C. representative. There must be at least one present at every show. That last solution does not happen nearly as often as it probably should.

The reader might well ask why the sport tends to become a battleground at this level. Think about it and you will realize we have talked about the elements before. Wealthy patrons want wins to bolster their egos. Professional handlers will not make a living for long at the sport if they lose. The people who pay them want results, not excuses. Dollars are very important! If you are not in the sport for money, that is your choice, says the professional. Do not cause problems for those who are. The dishonesty, viciousness, and pettiness of the sport all revolve around the dollars. Is it any different in other sports?

CHOOSING THE WINNER

The last round is coming up. Watch the other handlers. Do not let them grab an advantage here this close to the end. If there are any more dirty tricks, and there most certainly are, they will come now.

Some judges simply have everyone stack, then stroll the line and pick winners. Some do the same and send the entire field around a last time before selecting winners. Probably the most common scenario is for the judge to pull six to eight and have them move to a different part of the ring. If Lynnedora and Throck are "pulled," Lynnedora must listen to the judge very carefully. If the judge indicates a particular position he wants Throck to take, she must be sure she takes that position and holds it until the judge, if the judge ever does, instructs otherwise. If no instruction is given, she must place Throck where she will look better than the others in motion. Throck, in this example, is a Clumber. Wedging her between two setters would be an extremely bad choice.

Usually the judge dismisses those not pulled. He may then go over the animals again, send them out and back, stack them head on. This is all nothing for Throck or Lynnedora to be concerned about. They have done it all before and they've done it well, as their status now proclaims. It is certainly not a time to falter or get sloppy. Quite the contrary, it is a time for Throck to be on the jazz. The judge has probably already decided his placements and is confirming his conclusions. But then again, maybe the judge has not finalized. This is where it counts. The team, working as a team, must demand the win.

The judge sends his "pullouts" around singly and as a group. As the crowd applauds, the judge points to the first through fourth place winners. This is another time for Lynnedora to stay alert. Some judges will call out the breed. "First the Clumber. Second the Shorthair." Others simply point and shoot up fingers. Did the judge really point at the Clumber, or the Cocker just behind? If the Clumber handler hesitates, the pro on the Cocker will not. Now the judge will correct the mistake. But maybe, just maybe, especially for third or fourth place, the judge will not bother. After all, the quality of the two animals was close.

Lynnedora heard. The Clumber is number one. The winners take their places in front of the large numbers in the center of the ring that correspond to their placement. Remember, the contest ends when the ribbons are awarded. Until then, a judge could change the decision.

Once it is over, the handler who tried to step on Throck's foot and hide her from the judge will offer Lynnedora congratulations. Throck also deserves congratulations. She contributed as much or more to the win than Lynnedora.

A word of consolation, too, for those who do not win. You take your chances when you enter the contest. That is the name of this game. We all lose at times; most of us more than we win. Tomorrow you get another chance under different judges. Tomorrow could be your big win.

As to the winners, Lynnedora and Throck will get grudging admiration from those "in the know." If there is a male judge, a few may check to see if Lynnedora's blouse is low cut or her skirt short enough to show thigh. If the judge is a woman, they may suggest other possibilities. The pros will assure themselves it was a fluke, but they will worry every time they see Lynnedora and Throck appear to do battle.

Lynnedora should discreetly thumb her nose at the rumors and the rumor-mongers. She has that Group winning ribbon in her hand. Let the onlookers eat their hearts out. Do not linger for chit-chat and pictures now. There will be time for those later.

BEST-IN-SHOW

You still have one more contest to go. Since Throck took Group I in the Sporting Group, you are now obligated to enter her in the final contest of the day, which chooses the best animal in show.

Get Throck out of the sun and away from the crowd. (The winner of the last Group to compete will not get this opportunity, which certainly puts them at a disadvantage.) Give a treat, show some affection, and do as little grooming as possible. Both handler and animal rest and bond. Have a friend tell you when there are ten minutes to go.

The ten minutes are to exercise Throck, play, and put her back on the jazz. Next stop, the Best-in-Show ring.

There are only seven contestants this time, one team from each Group. As we see it, the judge of this contest has both the easiest and most difficult job of all. Bad dogs are not in this competition. The judge will once again appraise them and move them, but will probably not detect a serious fault. This contest will be won on heart.

Lynnedora can do little to help Throck now. She must only be careful to avoid detracting from her animal's performance. Throck will either take charge or she will not. She has the conditioning and stamina to enter the fray one last time, or she does not. If she has the heart of a Champion she will receive the only ribbon awarded in this contest — Best-in-Show.

We love happy endings, so we will create one for the reader. The judge sends each team around by itself and each receives the applause of those gathered. It is almost six o'clock now, still humid and warm. Win or lose, they are all superb animals, credits to their breed and group.

The Clumber is called next. Lynnedora takes a deep breath. "Come on, sweetheart," she says to Throck. "One more time, if you can."

Head lifts, neck arches, tail lifts and wags. With a look at her beloved handler, a smile if you will, Throck takes that first step. As she breaks into her gait, the rear legs power a little harder, the front legs reach that extra inch. There is no doubt in anyone's mind that she could do the job that Clumbers are bred for, to hunt the fields and heavy brush all day long. That animal knows it is her day. One last turn and she struts home.

The crowd quiets as the judge walks away from the contestants and moves to the table to record the winner's name and collect the trophy. Slowly the judge returns, flanked by the officers of the kennel club sponsoring the show, carrying flowers, trophy, and ribbon. The delegation moves in the direction of the little Pomeranian.

Mouths fall open. "A beautiful Pom, but we thought surely—," The judge stops, pauses, and changes direction. A hand reaches out and strokes the head of the Clumber bitch. It is over. Throckmortana is Best-in-Show.

Celebrate now, Lynnedora. Laugh, jump up and down, hug Throck, cry. Take lots of pictures! Give Throck a milkshake. There is nothing in this world that Throck loves more than a vanilla milkshake. Throck licks Lynnedora's face. Loves nothing more, except her family.

12.

Specialling

What a thrill when owner and animal taste that first success in the Group or Best-in-Show rings. People applauding, congratulating, and praising Throck. People you only casually know will deluge you with phone calls. Enjoy every second. No win is sweeter than the first.

When at last Lynnedora's moment ends, there are decisions confronting her. In all likelihood, well-meaning friends and at least a professional handler or two have already suggested Specialling.

It is not a decision to be made without a lot of thought — a lot of thought. We certainly would not presume to make the decision for her. But we would certainly not hesitate to point out some of the things that are worthy of consideration.

WHAT IS SPECIALLING?

Essentially it means entering your Champion in various shows with the *expectation* that he or she will vanquish the breed competition and will be eligible, therefore, to represent the breed in Group.

There are no guarantees. Everyone who competes has expectations, but only a small percentage are realized. We have more than once seen an open animal rise up and smite the specials. The open takes breed over the specials and leaves the special owners damning the judge. Less embarrassing, but no less defeating, is a loss to another special entered on the same day.

Lynnedora and Throck, because Throck is a bitch, are at risk in either situation. An excellent open male has a much better chance of going up over a bitch special than does the open bitch over a male special. That same open male will have problems defeating a quality dog special. A bitch special, by way of comparison, should not be surprised to lose to an open bitch or dog. That same special bitch will very likely lose to the male special.

That is not to say that Lynnedora should abandon the thought of Specialling Throck because she is a bitch. Although the road may be more difficult, bitches can and do prevail.

If Lynnedora decides to special Throck and enjoys success, she will then have to think about a more advanced and much more expensive step — campaigning. Campaigning is Specialling on a grand scale. Throck travels extensively, appearing in shows in many areas of the country, almost every week. Some campaigners appear in almost all of the major shows from New England to California. Other owners and/or handlers, preferring to be big fish in small ponds, enter their animals in small shows every week and only occasionally, depending on who is judging, make appearances at the larger shows.

WHY CAMPAIGN?

Why do people special and campaign their animals? There are as many reasons for campaigning as there are owners who do it. Not being privy to all those thoughts and dreams, we can only offer a few generalizations that we know to be true.

There are certain wealthy people who campaign dogs. In many cases, they obtain the dog from an owner/handler who lacks the means to campaign. The original owner sells the animal to a person of wealth with the stipulation that the animal will be returned after it is retired from competition.

The new owner then puts the animal out with a professional handler. The new owner pays all bills — entries, travel, maintenance, etc.; appears at shows, if at all, only when assured of acclaim and media coverage; claims a healthy tax write-off. In all the time he owns the animal, he may never get close enough to pet it.

Other animals embark upon the campaign trail to satisfy the ego of their owners. Like the parent who realizes his heretofore unrealized dream of sports stardom through the accomplishments of his child, many owners claim victories for themselves and ascribe losses to their animals. It is not uncommon to see the victorious animals hurriedly crated to allow owner and/or handler time to mix and mingle and accept applause. The next time you attend a show, watch what happens once the Group judge awards places. The handlers, most of them professionals, congratulate the winner's handler. The winner gets his picture taken. We always find it amusing that even the prizes are chosen with the owner in mind, never the animal. How many times have you seen a dog using a silver tea service?

Present, too, are those seeking financial reward. Eyebrows lift. How is that possible when clubs seldom offer cash prizes? When cash prizes are only token awards, at most?

Financial rewards are not always cash in hand. We have already mentioned those who invest to gain a tax write-off. Some owners see their animals being used in pet food commercials and on printed advertising. Certain companies have even leased Champions, which they then assign to a professional handler. Every time the animal wins, it is another plus for that food company. Little wonder owners sell their souls for such contracts. We are talking big dollars now, not tokenism.

Too, there are the breeders who hope to gain the financial rewards that will accrue to their kennels through those who wish to own the puppies of a multiple Group and/or Best-in-Show winner. As we mentioned in the section on breeding, a Champion parent is not a guarantee of the progeny's merit, but many people let ego rule over sense and insist on owning the child of Champions. Certainly the breeder needs this fallout. Whether breeding with the misguided goal of making a profit, or with the more inspirational intention of improving the breed, the program soon grinds to a halt when the puppies no longer sell and the financial drain plods ever onward and upward. Announcing to the world that you are breeding Champions, that you would have a potential buyer consider your animals before making a purchase, is a legitimate goal, if not an absolute necessity for breeders.

Believe it or not, among all the others, you will also find some few sportspersons. These are people who simply love the competition and who bring animals that share their enthusiasm for the sport. There are no elaborate preparations, devious schemes, accusations, or excuses. Both owner and animal come to compete, have fun together, renew old acquaintances, and then go home. Unfortunately, these last have become a rare breed. We can only assume that big money and politics, real or alleged, have driven these persons and their enthusiastic companions from the sport. Whatever the reason, their loss damages the sport beyond estimate.

We are not through yet. Keep in mind that we are trying to capture the reasons that thousands special and campaign their animals. Reducing those thousands of reasons into four or five very broad generalizations is not an easy task.

We cannot leave the subject without mentioning the hundreds of people who special animals, even campaign them, simply because of "kennel blindness." Many of them, perhaps most, do not even pretend to owning a kennel. They buy a purebred, hear about the sport, blunder in, and somehow, usually after many, many tries, realize a Champion. They are so in love with their animals that they are unable to see their faults, even the mediocrity. Certain that the world will be a better place for having been exposed to their beloved friend, they appear week after week, lose, and come back again. In their heart of hearts most of them believe that patience will triumph. Sooner or later a judge will see in the animal what the adoring owner sees. But sooner almost never comes and later comes only seldom. The chances that these animals will ever take a Group competition or Best-in-Show against the money, talent, quality, and politics arrayed against them equate with their chances of winning a lottery.

Before you decide where you fit and why you want to take on the challenge, consider a few factors that might decide your ability to take on the challenge. At the root of the matter is a single word — money.

PROFESSIONAL HANDLERS

"Should I attempt to handle my friend myself, or hire a professional handler?"

Certainly this is a problem to be addressed. Either way, it is expensive. If you are free to travel the country coast to coast, you have honed your handling skills, and you are willing to devote most of your time and energy to the sport, hug your friend and give it a go. If you cannot meet any or all of those criteria, you still want your friend campaigned, and you can face being without Throck for weeks at a time, hire a handler.

Do not, however, hire hastily. There are professional handlers and handlers who simply charge a fee for little in return. Talk to each at length to determine just exactly what they are prepared to offer you. There are those who will attempt to impress you with a list of judges they allegedly have in their pocket. Others will elaborate on a list of their victories. Those who should interest you are the ones who give the care of your animal priority, invite you to see their facility, arm you with a list of references, and describe their travel plans. Be at least as thorough in evaluating this person as you would be in evaluating an employee for your home or business. You may entrust the life and well-being of your friend to this handler.

Just as you expect to pay a highly accomplished employee a good sum for work in your company or home, you can also expect to pay a professional handler a lot for services rendered. There will be a fee for boarding, grooming, entry, travel, and showing. And these fees won't be small in any respect.

Before you reject the idea, compare the costs of hiring a professional to the costs of doing it yourself. You still have to board, feed, and groom. The entry fee is the same for you as for the handler. That leaves your overnight and traveling expenses. This can be expensive. Let's assume, for instance, that Lynnedora wants to attend one of the Houston clusters, Santa Barbara, or the Tar Heel Circuit in Carolina. These entail big logistics and big dollars. If she plans to attend one or more of the shows, she must first calculate travel time and add those days to the days consumed by the show.

TRAVELING TO SHOWS

But before she can calculate travel days, Lynnedora must decide how she intends to travel. The station wagon has worked so far, but does she want to put thousands of miles on what is already an aging vehicle? What does the family use for transportation while she is away?

It soon becomes clear that campaigning Throck may well require the purchase of a new vehicle. Another station wagon? That works, but it also means motels for every night on the road. Motels, in addition to expense, mean lugging crate, food, etc., in and out of motel rooms every night and morning on the road. Add to the motel costs the dollars spent at restaurants for fast food, haute cuisine, whatever will keep you going. The common element is that your choices will cost money.

Some people opt for a van. For multiple people and multiple animals, the extra room a van offers is an asset. If the weather is inclement, the van can be converted into a somewhat cramped grooming area. These are certainly assets to fill the positive side of the list. Now let's try the negative column. It costs a lot more than a station wagon. It costs more per mile to run it. Unless you are into roughing it and sleeping in the van and missing an occasional shower, the van solves neither the motel nor restaurant bills.

Some van owners attempt to rough it. They sleep in the van and, if at a showground without facilities, skip a shower or two. The hardy seem no worse for their weekend in the van. But then they are not campaigning an animal. On the campaign trail you will be out most every weekend. And some of these weekends may be four, five, even seven days long. It is an exhausting ordeal, at best, for both owner/handler and animal. Roughing it in a van is far from "at best." Grab all the comfortable beds, balanced meals, and warm showers you can get. Throck will not protest a little pampering between shows either.

Recreational Vehicles

Some of our friends (those with a good many extra dollars in their pockets) insist they have the answer to all problems posed by life on the campaign trail. Evidently many agree with those friends. Their solution — a motor home, or to be more generic, recreational vehicle. Judging by the number of such vehicles parked at even the small shows, the idea of traveling from show to show in such a vehicle is gaining in popularity.

A wise decision? We leave that for you to decide. We will, however, gladly share with you the information we have gathered and any thoughts that information has spawned.

One thing we can say with certainty is that any recreational vehicle — truck camper, travel trailer, motor home, fold-down trailer, multi-use vehicle—costs a whole lot more than five dollars, maybe too much more. We cannot help but think that we can pay a huge stack of motel bills and buy a thick stack of airline tickets for what a recreational vehicle would cost over the price of a station wagon. Of course, if you can convince the Internal Revenue Service to accept depreciation against taxes, that would help.

We mentioned all the categories of recreational vehicles above. As we see it, only the motor home would really solve the problems we also mentioned. A motor home affords you and your animal a reasonably comfortable place to sleep, bathe, and eat. In foul weather there is a spacious refuge and a warm, dry area to groom.

There is, too, the benefit of being able to arrive on the grounds early and park close to the action. Those of us who have carried eighty-pound, white animals through rain and mud from the grooming table to the ring, envy that easy access to the rings.

The community atmosphere that is shared by the owners of these vehicles during the off-hours can also be counted as a plus. Presumably everyone there loves dogs and the sport. With this commonality as a springboard, making new friends should be easy.

Sounds rosy, doesn't it? If you can afford motor homes, why not give one a go? Well, there are a few problems worth thinking about.

We mentioned the purchase price. Let's not overlook the cost of operation. Most of these adult toys only get six to ten miles per gallon. And if you break down? The Triple A will not be much help. There are some other organizations that specialize in helping those with recreational vehicles, but we leave it to you to investigate how extensive their coverage is and whether they will come to your assistance on those back roads that we often travel to and from the outdoor shows.

Those with experience tell us that there is more to moving these things from site to site than turning the key and steering the wheel. Careful attention must be given to proper loading. Weight distribution can make a difference in the handling, especially on a windy day. No one we interviewed described his vehicle as an aerodynamic marvel.

Many complain about the necessity for frequent gas stops. Unfortunately, these vehicles often come equipped with standard size gas tanks. With the fuel efficiency of these vehicles, it does not take long to empty a small tank.

When you arrive, hope that the showgrounds have the parking and hook-ups promised in the premium list you received. The individual clubs usually arrange the parking. Some clubs have a system, some think they have, others make no pretense. Add in a week of rain and even those clubs with the best pre-planning can give way to confusion.

Try to arrive at sites early, during daylight hours, if possible. Check the terrain carefully before you park. Club members, directing parking, are often more willing than capable. Make sure the area will support the vehicle in good and bad weather and that you can enter and exit without digging up the space. Continual site abuse will eventually prompt the owners to refuse motor homes. Remember that motel owners were receptive to dog people and their animals until they could no longer afford to be.

A dangerous aspect of motor home ownership is the threat of fire. Even more dangerous is the threat of multiple fires. Propane and carelessness combine for tragedy. When selecting that parking space, insist on leaving a good fifteen feet between your vehicle and those on either side.

We strongly suggest a practice run or two before investing in such an expensive addition as a motor home. There are people who lease. Experiment! Drive in bad weather. Argue with the handler who ropes off eight spaces that she is saving for friends. If, after a couple of trial runs, you are sold, happy motor homing.

Airplanes

There is another alternative. Whether you settle on station wagons and motels, vans and a sleeping bag, or a motor home, you will at times want to supplement your motor pool with an airplane. The United States is a very spacious country. To campaign in New England this weekend and California the next would test human, animal, and equipment, even if you have the time in between to make the drive. If both shows are a must, use an airplane.

Millions of dogs, owners, handlers, judges, and officials fly to shows every year. Usually they travel by air safely, but often not without incident. We certainly do not wish to mislead you. Flying to shows is expensive and requires renting transportation at the other end. When accompanied by an animal, the trip can be hectic and, for the animal, even dangerous. There are horror stories in abundance that tell of dead animals, lost animals, or misplaced reservations. Remember too that you must also arrange for your tack such as grooming table, box, etc., to be transported.

Again there are probably many ways of going about preparing for a tension-free, safe flight for Throck. Through the years we have probably borrowed from all of them. We offer you our system and invite you to amend it to your situation.

Start by purchasing a sturdy crate approved by the airlines. We use the fiberglass crates with a rib around the center, which assures that there will always be air space between the crate's vent and whatever is packed next to the crate. Some also use those crates for home use. We do not because they are more difficult to clean and provide greatly reduced air circulation in the summer compared to the standard cage-type crate. In any event, those airline-approved crates are available through many pet supply stores and may also be purchased at most airline terminals. While they're not free, the prices tend to be reasonable. One advantage for breeders — you can fly an animal to its new home and request the return of the crate United Parcel Service.

Also invest the time and expense to stop by the vet for a health certificate for Throck. Many areas require them as a prerequisite to your animal's entering or leaving their territory. Rather than try to memorize who wants what, attach the certificate to the top of the crate in a clearly marked envelope. Many airlines supply the envelope. If the certificate is required, it's there. One more thing is off your mind.

Call the airline and make your reservations *well* in advance. The airlines have rules limiting the number of live animals they may carry in a given space, plus or minus the quantity of other cargo. We have found that using a travel agent has its merits.

Make certain that whoever does the reservations makes it clear to the person on the other end that you will be accompanied by a live animal and excess baggage. Also give the animal's approximate weight. Though you can pay for your people ticket in advance, usually you must pay for the animal's at the airport when you check in. Plan to arrive at the airport well before flight time.

Since the dog's reservations are the important items, we usually call twice to confirm the reservations after we make them, the second time being the day before flying. It is better to hear the reservations are missing while there is still time to do something about it than to arrive at the airport, with animal, to learn they have no reservations for the animal or animals. Write down the date you place the reservations and the dates of confirmation. Also record the names of everyone you speak to.

Some other thoughts on scheduling the flight. If at all possible, select a non-stop flight. Unless they forget to load Throck at the point of origin (something that does happen and can be guarded against), there is no way for her to get off the plane or get mis-routed. Think of the panic at finding you are in Phoenix and Throck is in Seattle.

Because such mis-routings can and do happen, to luggage and animals, when connecting flights are involved, avoid them. What if you cannot? Whether a direct flight or connecting, we request permission to speak to the person who will load Throck. It has been our experience that the airline is most cooperative. They certainly do not want anything to happen to Throck either. We have accompanied our animals to the fringe of the tarmac. We ask the person to keep Throck out of dangerous heat or cold, as the case may be, as much as possible before loading. This is a reasonable request to which they take no offense.

We also request that they contact the terminal or the pilot with a confirmation that Throck is loaded. This request does a double service since we advise the crew that we will not board and/or fly until Throck's loading is confirmed. It also alerts the pilot that live animals are on board and reminds him to make certain that the compartment carrying Throck is pressurized and temperature controlled. The airline's cooperation is not always as readily extended in the instance of loading confirmation, but it happens if you stand firm. Remember, only you can assure Throck's safety and speak for her.

We try to relieve the weather threat by scheduling late night and early morning flights. What weather problems? Ask Throck to describe life on the tarmac, in a crate, when temperatures are torrid or below freezing. Many of the horror stories trace back to this critical time period.

Twelve hours before departure, give or take a little, we stop Throck's food and water. She then gets nothing to eat or drink until arrival. That includes tranquilizers. If your animal needs to be tranquilized to travel on a plane, stay home. Except in cases of extreme cold or puppies on long flights, we also refrain from adding any bedding. If the exceptional conditions prevail, we prefer cedar shavings.

Once all is ready, and usually while waiting for the luggage person to collect the animal, we affix clearly printed cards to all four sides and top of crate. These cards contain our name, address, home phone, and phone where we will be staying in the place of destination.

We have lost luggage while flying, but we've never lost our live animal luggage. Other than an annoyed ground attendant or two, we and our animals have flown problem-free. Not everyone has been as fortunate. Take the time to do it right. A dead animal cannot do it over.

By now, I am sure that you understand our point when we say that campaigning an animal is *very* expensive. As we mentioned earlier, it is so expensive that some owners of moderate means will sell their animals to wealthy patrons looking for tax benefits because they simply cannot afford to finance a campaign themselves. The animal is then sold back to the original owner after the campaign. The owners assure us that they sacrificed their own feelings and sent the dog off to a sponsor for the good of the animal.

ADVERTISING YOUR DOG

Travel, food, lodging, entry fees, or professional handlers' fees if you so choose—all these add up to lots of money. But it is not the end. There is yet another major area of expense. Advertising!

Those who go to the expense of campaigning their animal do not want to trust to the fates to whisper the results to dogdom. If their animal, who gets points for every dog beaten in Group and Best-in-Show, is ranked number one in its breed nationally, or in the top ten of all breeds nationally, these owners also are unwilling to wait for the results to be published in A.K.C. awards three months hence and then take the chance that important judges will *see* those results in the magazine.

Full-page ads in dog magazines, weekly dog newspapers, and breed publications are the ticket. Place them wherever vanity is served and they might be seen by the judges. Many of these publications are automatically sent to each and every judge in the United States and Canada each and every week. It costs big dollars to print a photo of a big-name judge awarding victory ribbons to animal and handler. They look in every respect like the hundreds of ads before them picturing big-name judges giving awards to animal and handler. Please do not try anything original.

As we mentioned, the dog on the campaign trail competes against every other dog in the country for ranking. There are several ranking systems built around points awarded for various levels of victory. Never having had the top-rated animal in the country on any of the rating systems, we can only guess what emotional highs result. We have to suppose that the money, time, and energy spent on each inch of the high was worth it. To those owners, our congratulations.

One more person should be consulted about the price of campaigning. Do you suppose Throck has any conception of rankings? If she does, would she willingly dedicate a third to a half of her life, most of it in crates, traveling hither and yon, often with someone other than the pack leader and beloved pack? At least twice each week Throck is led to the amphitheater to perform against strange animals, to the applause of strange humans. What would Throck say? Given a choice, would the dog willingly make those physical and emotional sacrifices for a ranking?

And if the dog remains unranked? Does she suffer the agony of defeat? Or is she satisfied to know that the other campaigners spent more money? Would the dog do it all again knowing that her sacrifices gained her absolutely nothing? Well, not nothing. Think what each victory did for the ego of owner and handler.

A negative note on which to end the subject of campaigning. The temptation is to leave the discussion there, but that would not be quite fair. Super animals do come along, and it is fortunate when they are owned or sponsored by those who can afford to share the greatness of that animal with dog lovers around the world. When and if that super animal results from our breeding program, we would certainly hope that we could afford to campaign him around the country and let as many people as possible experience that heart flutter one experiences in the presence of the superior animal.

We would hope, however, that should the occasion arise, we would not lose perspective. The point we wanted to make above and wish to drive home here is that the animal is the star, not the owner, and not the sponsor. Campaign as long as the tail keeps wagging. The first time the animal appears less than enthusiastic, or the tail flutters and stops, pack without delay and go home! Give a walk in the park, a roam across a field, hugs and kisses, treats. The special animal gave his loved ones everything he had for as long as he could. Now is the time to rejuvenate his spirit with a steady flow of love and affection from human to animal.

13.

The International Challenge

There are always more mountains to climb. Campaigning a Champion in the United States is not enough challenge for some owners. They wish to see their animal's name and the wall of their trophy room adorned with international titles. The opportunities are there. For those with the means to launch such a campaign, there are competitions all around the world.

What follows is not an exhaustive list of all the international competitions. There is, for example, a show circuit each year in Bermuda. It is a completely enjoyable experience, so we have heard, but we know little more about it than that. The Bermuda circuit is one for the reader to investigate.

Keep in mind also that the rules of the game may vary greatly from U.S. competitions. To the extent that we know of such changes, we will advise you here. We strongly recommend, however, that you use our information only as a springboard. Investigate thoroughly before investing in a trip.

NORTH AMERICA

The Caribbean

Let's start close to home with the Caribbean and branch out from there. Puerto Rico, of course, is a commonwealth of the United States. A.K.C. prevails over the sport there and their shows follow the same format as other A.K.C. shows. Language will prove only a small problem, as most in the San Juan area speak enough English to communicate. Watch the heat and humidity. Keep the shade and cool water handy. The big animals who suffer in heat will not enjoy a warm day at sea level. (See *The Road to Westminster* for first aid strategies.)

The Bahamas Kennel Club also offers a two-day show each year in Nassau. Though we can find no specific information on the Nassau show's requirements, we would suggest three items for any trip outside the country. First, a rabies shot for the animal. Second, a vaccination and health certificate for the accompanying human. Third, check to see if an Import License is required. (The Import License is simply a vehicle for the host to charge a tax.) A travel agent or the A.K.C. should be able to confirm or deny the need for an import license, how to get one, and when you need it. Those who prevail can come away with a Bahamian Championship and a good suntan.

Mexico

Since we have our warm weather gear, let's stop off in Mexico. Several shows are held in this nation each year. For a schedule, write to the Federacion Canofilia Mexicana A.C. (See the appendix for the address.) In addition to the paperwork mentioned, be prepared to prove that your animal is also protected against Distemper, Parvo, Hepatitis, and Leptospirosis.

Do not travel to Mexico expecting to come away with a Championship in one weekend against inferior competition. Your competition will at least be clean and well groomed and probably of better than average quality. In place of ribbons, the judges hand out colored cards. Read your card carefully. If the judge has checked the "very good" or "excellent" box on the card, your animal qualifies for breed honors. The judge will also indicate on your card whether he believes your animal worthy of a Championship point. Where an A.K.C. Championship can be won under two different judges, the Mexican version must be won under four different judges. And there are no child phenomenons such as we experience in the States. Cute puppies, even sensational puppies, must demonstrate that their virtues continue into adulthood. In Mexico, at least two championship points must be earned after the animal reaches fifteen months of age. In this we applaud the Mexican wisdom.

Canada

Off to our neighbor on the north — Canada. It sounds easy enough, but it is not all that easy. Canada requires exacting paperwork, started months before the shows you plan to attend. In January you should write to The Canadian Kennel Club (see appendix) and request a non-resident application, along with a nose printing kit. That's not a misprint — one nose printing kit. You might also want to request a booklet appropriately entitled *Dog Show Rules*.

Do all the paperwork carefully because they charge for correcting errors. Complete the application and return it. In the same envelope, include a three generation pedigree and an A.K.C. registration. The pedigree must be the official version issued by A.K.C. and the registration must be the original. Include also two quality nose prints, taken per the instructions that come with the kit. Complete your application with a money order for the amount requested, probably twenty to twenty-five Canadian dollars. If the exchange rate is favorable to the U.S., as it is at this writing, have the person selling the money order discount it.

If you have completed the requirements you will eventually receive a membership in the Canadian Kennel Club. That membership becomes extremely important if you finish a championship and still have shows to attend. You may not upgrade your animal to special if you are not a member of the Club.

The membership also includes a subscription to the official *Dogs in Canada*, which is an important addition to your library. Unlike the version that goes out to the general public, the official version advises members about impending shows and judging panels.

Now you're on your way. With the membership in your pocket, proof of recent rabies vaccination and description of the dog ready to show at the border, it's away to Canada.

If you read the book of rules you should have noted that there are differences between the Canadian shows and the U.S. shows. In Canada, an animal only needs ten points for a championship. Though no majors are required, Throck must go winners under three different judges. If Throck is Winner's bitch, she wins the bitch points. If she is Best of Winners, add the dog's points to the bitch points. That does not mean she gets the larger of the two amounts, as it does in the States. It means she gets both amounts. With one catch. She cannot win more than five points at any one show.

The other major difference is at Group level. In the U.S., those who take breed are invited to the Group competition. But many times in the U.S., Breed winners, for reasons of their own, head home before Group competition. Whether driven away by the politics of the Group ring or the lateness of the hour, they leave. Do not do that in Canada. If you win Breed, you are required to stay for the Group competition. Failure to do so forfeits all points and titles earned at that show and further disciplinary action may be given as determined by the C.K.C.

Most Americans enjoy Canadian shows. Most see them as less tension-provoking than A.K.C. shows.

EUROPE

Well, where next? Perhaps you have a trip planned and want to include a run at a Championship. How about Europe?

Unless you plan a very long stay, cross the English shows off your dream list. What's the problem? England, to protect the island from rabies, insists that all dogs arriving from other lands be quarantined for six months. That's a long time for your friend to live in a kennel under the care of strange people, in addition to being more than quite expensive.

Ireland, with its pubs, the tenors, the Blarney stone? No luck here, either; the same quarantine is in effect, as it is in Scotland also.

The mainland is more receptive, with the exception of Finland, Sweden, and Norway. They, too, have quarantines, though they are only four months in duration.

If you're armed with a health certificate, vaccination certificate, and proof of a recent rabies vaccination, the other European countries will welcome you and Throck. Wait, that's not quite true. Spain wants you to show that Throck is also protected against Hepatitis and Parvovirus. To that list add Panleukopenia and Kennel Cough for Yugoslavia.

The Federation Cynologique Internationale, headquartered in Belgium (see appendix), is the governing body for all European shows. Again we urge you to use our information only as a starting point. Write to the F.C.I. for definitive answers to the many questions we will undoubtedly leave unanswered.

Once you and Throck arrive in Europe, traveling with your animal is a much more pleasant experience than traveling with your animal in the United States. Perhaps a better word than pleasant would be civilized. After all, dogs are people too.

In Europe, with few exceptions, you may sightsee where you will, eat and sleep where you will, and travel where you will, always with Throck at your side. Of course Throck will be expected to be well-mannered. With no intention to mislead you, there are hotels, restaurants, beaches, and trains that prohibit or restrict dogs. There are at least as many hotels, restaurants, beaches, and trains that welcome animals.

We do not wish to tire our readers by describing every nuance of every European country's show. One example, however, should demonstrate that the game changes in Europe. Those who aspire to challenge are well advised to investigate thoroughly and prepare accordingly.

France

The French shows serve well to make our point. An American, used to A.K.C. shows, might well be shocked walking into a French dog competition in progress.

The French are much more casual in their approach than Americans. Be prepared to see some judges who remain seated while they assess the contestant. Handlers chat freely with each other and make little or no attempt to control, let alone pose, their dogs while waiting to be judged. Children and friends do not hesitate to enter the ring and spend time with the contestants and their owners. If that's not casual enough, the spectators outside the ring frost the cake. They shout encouragement to individual animals, whistle, and offer bait. It goes without saying that there is no enforced penalty for double handling in France.

Dogs are categorized into ten groups in France as compared to seven here. It is strange that they bother to group at all in light of the fact that they have no Group competition or Best-in-Show.

Once you and your animal adjust to the new environment, be prepared for a completely different award system. You first must determine whether you are at a national show or an international show. In either case, you will have to enter one of four classes — Champion, Working, Open, or Junior.

At an international show, in France or elsewhere in Europe, the highest certificate awarded is Certificat d'Aptitude au Championnat de Beauté. After the judge appraises each dog, the entire entry circles the ring. Starting with the least award, Assez Bon, the judge will pull people out of the parade. When they leave, he next stops those who are entitled to the Bon, the award given for good type with faults. Next is the Tres Bons, those that have fewer faults. Finally the Excellent is presented. If there is more than one, the judge arranges them into First Excellent, Second Excellent, etc.

With a First Excellent, Throck would probably also win a Certificat d'Aptitude au Championnat International de Beauté, but that does not necessarily follow. The judges may withhold that award.

If Throck does walk away with one, she is a fourth of the way to her International Championship. The next three have to be won in at least two other countries under at least two other judges.

It is a similar situation with the national shows in France, in which the award sought is the Certificat d'Aptitude au Championnat National de Beauté.

The ultimate contest in France is the Paris show. Only animals with Certificats d'Aptitude or Championships from other areas may enter. To take it a step further, owners of working and sporting dogs must show evidence of their animal's ability to perform that activity for which it was bred. (If the A.K.C. instituted that rule, a large proportion of the Working and Sporting dogs would disappear from the events in the states.) Throck, for instance, being a Clumber Spaniel and a Sporting dog, would have to have her entry supported with a field trial certificate. The plum of the Paris show is the Champion de Beauté de France.

THE FAR EAST

We think it is safe to say that it's not quite as easy to become a Champion in Europe as it is in the United States. Perhaps you would prefer to travel west instead and try your luck in the Far East.

Because Japan and the Philippines are the only full members of the Federation Cynologique Internationale, the same ruling board we met in Europe, most of the important shows are held in Manila or Tokyo. Do not plan a rest stop in Hawaii on the way, since the quarantine for dogs is four months long.

There is no quarantine in the Philippines if all the animal's papers are in order. Be prepared to offer a health certificate and vaccination certificate and to pay for an Import License. They also require a long list of shots—Parvovirus, Kennel Cough, Rabies, Hepatitis, Panleukopenia, Distemper, and Leptospirosis.

Though Japan requires only a vaccination and health certificate, along with a rabies shot, if you choose Japan you'll need to arrive at least two and a half weeks early. Japan does have a fourteen day quarantine.

A Japanese version of a dog show is what one has come to expect from the Japanese — it is efficient and controlled. It closely parallels an A.K.C. version. About the only differences in classes occur when the judge awards a breed ribbon to the best puppy, older puppy, young adult, etc. All of these breed winners then compete in Group. The system makes for bigger groups, but ultimately only the seven top animals compete for Best-in-Show. (Not to mislead the reader, although the Japanese have seven groups, they are not the same seven as in the U.S. There, herding and working are still one. The seventh group in Japan offers Japanese national dogs, i.e., Chin, Akita, and many breeds not recognized by the A.K.C.)

Lynnedora would have no trouble orienting and scheduling since much of the literature, including the all-important catalog, appears in both Japanese and English. She might, however, be surprised the first time she sees two or three breeds being judged in the same ring, at the same time, by different judges.

The biggest surprise awaiting the American entry is that an animal must pass a breed surveyor or an intended function test, similar to that mentioned in France, before qualifying to enter. (Does it surprise the reader to realize that only Americans have trouble accepting the notion that a sporting dog is not a true Champion if she cannot perform that for which she was bred?)

Plan to stay in Japan a good while. For a Japanese Championship, the animal must accumulate twenty points, including three major points. The catch is that major points, as we understand it, can only be earned at the few important shows held each year.

THE WORLD SHOW

For those who wish an International Championship of repute, yet cannot afford to travel hither and yon for long periods, perhaps you would do well to set your sights on the World Show. It is the ultimate show among those who vie for Championships recognized by our friends from the Federation Cynologique Internationale, and it is held in a different country each year.

If you and your animal seek one opportunity to make your mark on the sport in the international arena, the World Show is the place to do it. Though it is run much like the French show we described, a few warnings are in order.

Realize first that there may be as many as ten thousand dogs entered. Remember that people outside the ring can shout, whistle, cavort, and openly double handle. Understand that such contests, with competitions among animals of different countries, are viewed by the Europeans, at least, as a scaled-down version of the World Cup or the Olympics. Competition often is less than genteel.

Again we applaud the F.C.I. for requiring their judges to give a written critique of each animal judged. Should your animal lose after traveling all that distance, you will at least know why the judge put your animal down and you will not have to guess, as we do in the States. Requiring judges to write a judicious critique and animals to demonstrate proof of their breed intention would certainly revolutionize the sport as we know it here and perhaps rid it of some of its bad qualities.

14.

Specialties

We did it once again! After a conservative introduction to the major league of the sport, we jumped from the Group and Best-in-Show competitions to a maximum program that has Throck being expensively campaigned from one side of the country to the other and on to International competition.

CAN YOU AFFORD THE CAMPAIGN TRAIL? __

Though we cannot afford such an elaborate challenge, there are a surprising number of people who can and do. Some professional handlers tour the world, deriving their entire income for the year. A partial domestic campaign can cost $25,000 a year to an owner-handler.

"We cannot do it," Lynnedora complains. "We love the sport and want to see Throck recognized as the best animal in the sport, but those expenditures are way out of our reach."

Here is a dilemma! If there are those like Lynnedora, who entered the sport as a family project and cannot afford to travel hither and yon, how can they ever hope to see their animal recognized as the best?

Lynnedora sincerely believes that on any given day Throck could defeat any dog in the world and enjoy doing it. Do she and the family just throw up their hands and fold their tent? There is a good possibility they will never have the money for such an elaborate campaign. If they must always abort their challenge at this juncture, should they consider cancelling their breeding program and dropping out of the sport? Many, frustrated and without seeing a light at the end of the tunnel, have done just that.

You do not want to have made serious expenditures and invested much labor, only to have it all end in a wash of frustration. There is a way — a good, realistic, only moderately expensive way.

The Champion of the campaign trail — the animal who appears in full page ads, has amassed thousands of points, and has an International Championship or two — that animal, with all its credentials, cannot yet claim to be the best in this or any other country. Until that animal can show a win at the National Specialty of its breed and then take the brass ring at the big one, at Westminster, it is not the best.

The strategy follows. Let them spend their thousands and amass their credits. The pressure is on them to win a Specialty. They cannot be the best without defeating the best of their own breed. And having done that, they must triumph at Westminster, against other mega-point animals and lesser knowns, with names like Throck. To borrow from Yogi Berra, "It's not over 'til it's over," or words to that effect.

The strategy, we are happy to say, is straightforward, and only limitedly a tax on assets. The key word here is focus. There are two goals. If Throck can go to Westminster off a National Specialty win, she will have a credit that many of the big winners could only hope for. She is a force to be feared. That is goal one.

A NATIONAL SPECIALTY

Let's focus and not get ahead of ourselves. Goal one. There is a National Specialty coming up. That competition is the focus.

What is a National Specialty?

A National Specialty is, in many ways, just another dog show. In fact, they are often held in conjunction with all breed shows. Yet there is an important distinction. A National Specialty is a contest restricted to a single breed. The very best representatives of that Breed, puppies to geriatrics, aspiring to long-since Champions, converge to contest for the honor of being pronounced Best-of-Breed.

"Best of Breed," says Lynnedora. "Is that all there is? It doesn't sound like a lot against a string of Bests-in-Show and International wins."

If a Best-of-Breed win at a National Specialty does not sound like much, then you are not listening carefully. As we said, a National Specialty attracts representatives of a single breed to contest each other. They come from all over the country. Many times there is a sweepstakes competition, previous to classes, at which the entrants can win money. After deciding Best-of-Breed and the Awards of Merit, a Stud Dog and Brood Bitch competition is held. The stud enters the ring with up to three of his progeny, and his stud prowess is evaluated by evaluating his progeny. The stud with the best quality progeny wins. Likewise the dam with the best get. Remember, the parent is not judged, only the progeny.

Usually the festivities are capped by a parade of Champions. One more time legends of the breed circle the ring to the applause of those who remember.

Sounds like fun, doesn't it? A chance to see and compete against the best animals in the breed; to meet the best breeders; to learn from the best handlers. It is fun. It is also inspirational and educational. No book on the breed can ever capture the combined experience of those assembled.

Lynnedora has started breeding. She owes it to herself to attend and see what others have bred and hear their triumphs and disasters. It is a chance for her to decide what she likes and choose a direction. With luck she will see three and four generations of several lines.

The Competition Itself

Now to the competition. The best of the breed from every corner of the country participates. When Lynnedora takes Throckmortana into the ring for the Best-of-Breed competition, she will be challenged by forty, fifty, or more Champions. She will never encounter competition of the like at a regular all-breed show.

We are certainly impressed by any animal that can take a Group placement at an all-breed show. A Best-in-Show is sensational, even fantastic. But these victories pale in comparison with a specialty win. If Throckmortana wins there, she is truly a Champion of Champions.

There is one piece of unfinished business. When the Specialty is held in isolation, without affiliation with an all-breed show, the day ends for the class dogs and Champions with the awarding of the Best-of-Breed and Awards of Merit (honorable mentions). Those who participate in a Specialty as part of an all-breed show, however, if they have any emotion or energy left, can continue to Group and so on, as usual.

Once again, we underline this option. For the owner who simply cannot afford the time, travel, and advertising costs demanded by the campaign trail, concentrate on a win at a Specialty. If Throck cannot fill her wall with trophies, she should concentrate on one of the two trophies that outshine them all.

PREPARING FOR THE SPECIALTY

What we suggest, in the meantime, is for Lynnedora, Throck, and the family to stay in rhythm, finely tuned for the Specialty. A return to basics could be very beneficial. A review of all the little things they think they are still doing, the very things that took Throck to her Championship, may well turn up a thing or two that has slipped in quality, or has even disappeared.

The team should also go over all the equipment, supplies, and tack. Repair and refurbish anything that needs it. Going to a show as a class act is good for everyone's confidence. A class act also jangles the confidence of the competition.

To stay tuned, Lynnedora should enter her friend in nearby shows that require small investments of time and money. It will be important for the whole team to attend these shows, reestablish their teamwork, hone the ring skills, and cement friendships.

Avoid the long trips, the motel stays, and the restaurant meals. Instead, have fun, rejuvenate the spirit, and polish what you do best. No stress and no strain is permitted.

That does not mean the team should not remain competitive. If you are at the show, go for it. A few more group placements and a Best-in-Show win or two would certainly go well with the National Specialty win.

Remember the key word — focus. Everything you do from now to the Specialty should contribute to that effort. Experiment, practice, err now. We want the team to hit the Specialty on the run and sweep to victory before the others know what hit them.

Make no mistake. With a National Specialty win to her credit, Throckmortana automatically joins the elite.

15.

Westminister

Whatever you may hear to the contrary, there is no win in the sport that compares with Best-in-Show at Westminster. There are larger shows, perhaps even prettier shows, but none that compares in prestige. Westminster is the end of the rainbow, the glorious destination that lies at the end of the yellow brick road. For our purposes, we shall call it Focus Two.

If we said anything along the way to mislead the readers into believing that the Road to Westminster is either easy or short, we apologize. The road is often difficult, discouraging, even heartbreaking; it can be very, very, very long. Ch. Covey Tucker Hills Manhattan, for instance, was eight years old before he prevailed.

At the same time, we hasten to add that the road offers fun and satisfaction to those who plan ahead and allow themselves the luxury of enjoying life. Watch your four-legged friend. As long as the tail keeps wagging, march on.

Perhaps the greatest problem facing the first-time entrant at Westminster is something called intimidation. In addition to all the things we said and meant about the show's prestige, it's in New York City — an intimidating place for many people. No wonder the novice feels intimidated.

Well, throw off that cloak of fear. In spite of all the adjectives, essentially Westminster is only another dog show. It is the same game, with frills. Judges, animals, hopeful owners and handlers, spectators— you have seen many of them at other shows, competed against them, and won. Only the buildings and ambiance changes.

ATTEND WITHOUT THE DOG FIRST _____

Still, if you have any reservations, we strongly recommend that you and family and/or friends attend your first Westminster without Throck. We do not want to minimize the difficulty of the logistics. New York is not an open field ten miles outside Cleveland.

Structure your trip to simulate the one you will take next year with Throck. Will you drive, fly, or take the train? What equipment will you take? How will you get yourself, animal, and tack to the hotel, then to Madison Square Garden?

One difference from all but six or seven other shows is that Westminster is a benched show. There is nothing to fear in that. At a benched show each animal is allotted a prescribed space. (Check with A.K.C. or your Club to determine the space allotted to your breed. You may have to purchase a smaller crate than Throck uses at home.) The animal and handler must arrive at a prescribed time on the day of your scheduled judging. The show is always held on a Monday and Tuesday just prior to Valentine's Day in February. Someone must stay with the animal at all times, even though it is crated, to answer the questions posed by any of the hundreds of spectators. Both animal and handler, unlike the situation at other shows, must remain until the cessation of activities for the day.

Devise a plan to cover all the little things you would normally do at a show; allowing Throck to empty her bladder, or dump, for example. There are areas for this purpose inside the building. What do you do outside the building? These are the streets of New York.

Pick a hotel listed in the premium list for Westminster. Whether you stay there this trip or not, drop by, check out the entrances, and inquire as to the hotel's rules regarding Throck.

One important matter that we should mention before we forget. Next year, when you plan to enter Throck, do so as soon as you receive the premium list. This show has a limited entry, usually around 2,500. The quota fills quickly—within days. We do not want you to anticipate and make expensive plans only to have your entry returned.

Spend as much time at the show as you can. Watch a variety of competitions; study the techniques of proficient handlers from all over the country. It is a great opportunity to take notes on the likes and dislikes of the judges and the format they employ. The more you immerse yourself in the activities and meet and enjoy old friends, animal and human, the sooner the intimidation factor will fade away.

IN THE RING

That is not to say that a small lump will not clutch the chest on Tuesday evening. Gowns, tuxedos, the glitter of jewelry, flowers will fill the place. The finest animals in the world, accompanied by the best handlers in the world (not all professionals), march into the ring to be judged by the most knowledgeable judges in the world. No jostling and jockeying for position is permitted here. The space allotted each contestant is clearly marked with the name of the breed. The tails are wagging. An animal must have at least one championship point to enter, so all have performed before.

Under the scrutiny of hundreds of spectators and the glare of television lights, legends and novices give it their best. Win or lose, each team is a Champion.

Almost too soon, one animal and one handler stand in the spotlight. Best-in-Show at Westminster. Close your eyes and allow yourself the dream. Yes, we can see it too: Lynnedora, with her arms around her friend. The end of the rainbow. The last stop on the yellow brick road. No matter how many years they spend in the sport, there will never be another win like it. For one shining moment, they are the best in the world.

16.

Is There a Morning After?

Because we wrote the book, we could let Throck win this year, or next. Focus Two pays off. The bitch takes down the International Champion and stands for one brief moment as the best in the world. It can happen that way. It won't always, but it can.

A NEW PUPPY

And the next day, or the next week, what is left for Lynnedora, Throck, and the family? They possess the brass ring.

It is all left. Yesterday is over, Westminster is over, and it is all there to do again. One experience down, many to go over the years.

For Lynnedora and her family there is much to do. They have another little girl coming along. They need to get her out and let her experience the world, socialize her as a preparation for her show career.

Walk the baby on different surfaces and through water. Do not force results, this is adventure time. Stairs and ramps provide a challenge. So do doggy doors, especially if they open onto a tunnel that penetrates the house wall. Play ball with the baby, it's great for her coordination. Stand her on the grooming table and brush her.

On an especially brave day, put her and crate on your dolly and take her for a ride. Load her and crate into the vehicle and take her to town. Try a little lead walking. No obedience training, however; not yet. Above all else, do not forget the vanilla milkshake.

WHAT'S NEXT FOR THROCK?

Is Throck's nose out of joint because the puppy, her daughter, is getting all the attention? Well, she does not have to join the geriatric sector quite yet. She should retire from conformation. As Specialty winner and Best-in-Show winner at Westminster, she has stood atop the mountain. There is no place higher she can climb.

But conformation is not the be-all and end-all in the sport. It may be the most glamorous aspect, but there are many other challenges available.

There is obedience competition, for example. Dog and handler working together, competing as a team against themselves for yet another Championship. It is a wonderful bonding experience for both animal and human. Depending on the breed you own, there are several other possibilities that invite the whole family. What a wonderful thing for the sport if owners would give their friends the opportunity to use the instincts that were bred into them.

For sporting dogs, there are field trials. Pointing, flushing, and retrieving. If you own a rabbit dog — a beagle, basset, dachshund — there are plenty of tracking contests for them.

Lure coursing provides competition opportunities for the sighthounds. They get to let it all hang out in pursuit of that elusive rabbit and are scored on their efforts.

Dogs with discerning noses can participate in a tracking competition for them. Those who excel in scent discrimination over a prescribed course can earn yet another title — Tracking Dog, TD. Not enough challenge? Then put that nose on a five-hour-old course and let your animal take home a TDX.

Working dogs, many of them anyway, love to pull. If they are Nordic types, let them try the sled races.

The herders can find several competitions. Some use eye, others bark, still others stalk. The object is the same. Whether the club uses ducks and geese, or large animals, the animal competes against others in gathering and bringing home.

We think you have the point. Without laboring the subject, there are many opportunities for humans and breeds. Look into Den Trials, Canine Good Citizenship, Agility, Search and Rescue.

It is time to leave Lynnedora and her family to reflect on their experience at leisure, remember good things and bad, make decisions. They know now they have several choices.

Whatever they decide, we hope they include the whole pack and that all will enjoy it. Having fun is not the only game in town, but it is the best game. For now, we leave them with this advice. Make certain the tail keeps wagging.

Appendix I

GLOSSARY OF DOG SHOW TERMS

Angulation. Usually refers to angle at which bones meet at the joint in hip; the stifle to hock configuration.

Arm Band. Cardboard number displayed on left arm during competition.

Bait. Anything used to gain favorable response from a dog. Ranges from food to toys.

Balance. Symmetrical proportions.

Backskull. Back of head.

Benched Show. Animals are displayed on benches for entire show.

Bite. Relationship of upper to lower teeth.

Chalking. Use of any foreign substance to alter dog's natural color.

Cheek. Part of head below eye and behind mouth.

Close Behind. Hocks are close together when moving.

Close Coupled. Too little length of back from last rib to hip.

Cobby. Too short-bodied.

Cow-hocked. Hocks turn toward each other when moving, while feet turn out.

Crabbing. Moves with rear feet outside front feet, or at angle with straight line.

Croup. The last part of the back before the tail.

Double Handling. A person known to the dog positions himself outside the ring and helps handler keep animal up, on the jazz.

Down in Pastern. Weak front ankles.

Drive. Action of rear legs pushing dog forward.

Elbow. Joint between lower and upper front arms.

Elbowing Out. Elbows turn out as dog moves, rather than staying close to sides.

Expression. A look that implies intelligence.

Fault. A defect in terms of breed standard.

Feathering. The fringe on ears, tail, and legs.

Finished. Animal has amassed enough points and majors to claim Championship.

Flews. Overlapping lips.

Furnishing. See Feathering.

Gait. The animal's natural pattern of moving comfortably.

Gay Tail. Tail carried above back line.

Hackney. A high, affected-looking front reach. Overdone.

Haw. A third lid on inside of eye.

Height. Always measured from withers to ground.

Hocks. Rear ankle.

Layback. Angle of front shoulder in relation to forearm.

Leather. The exterior ear.

Leggy. Legs are too long.

Level Bite. Upper and lower teeth meet exactly.

Loin. Area from last rib to rump.

Low-set. Ears on side of head and/or tail attached below back line.

Occiput. Most raised portion of backskull.

Overshot. Upper teeth far overlapping lower teeth in front.

Pacing. Both legs on a side move at same time in the same direction.

Paddling. Forelegs do not provide proper lift.

Pastern. Joint between ulna and radius.

Reach. The amount of forward stride by the forelegs.

Rib Spring. Full, rounded rib presentation as opposed to slab sides.

Scissors Bite. Upper teeth overlapping, but still showing lower teeth in front.

Sound. A well structured, smooth moving, healthy animal.

Special. An animal competing in Best of Breed that has already completed its Championship.

Stacking. Posing the animal to present a balanced outline.

Sternum. Chest.

Steward. A person appointed to assist the judge in the ring.

Stifle. The rear knee.

Stop. A distinct step from nose to head.

String Up. Pose and/or move dog on tight lead. (To lift dog's front.)

Swayback. A back that sags in the middle.

Topline. The back.

Tuck Up. Belly slopes up to loin.

Typey. Very close to proper look of breed as described in standard.

Undershot. Lower teeth overlap upper teeth in front.

Withers. Highest part of body found just behind the neck.

Appendix II

BREEDS RECOGNIZED BY THE AMERICAN KENNEL CLUB

SPORTING GROUP
Brittanys
Pointers
Pointers (German Shorthaired)
Pointers (German Wirehaired)
Retrievers (Chesapeake Bay)
Retrievers (Curly-Coated)
Retrievers (Flat-Coated)
Retrievers (Golden)
Retrievers (Labrador)
Setters (English)
Setters (Gordon)
Setters (Irish)
Spaniels (American Water)
Spaniels (Clumber)
Spaniels (Cocker)
Spaniels (English Cocker)
Spaniels (English Springer)
Spaniels (Field)
Spaniels (Irish Water)
Spaniels (Sussex)
Spaniels (Welsh Springer)
Vizslas
Weimaraners
Wirehaired Pointing Griffons

HOUND GROUP
Afghan Hounds
Basenjis
Basset Hounds
Beagles
Black and Tan Coonhounds
Bloodhounds
Borzois
Dachshunds
Foxhounds (American)
Foxhounds (English)
Greyhounds
Harriers
Ibizan Hounds
Irish Wolfhounds

Norwegian Elkhounds
Otterhounds
Petit Basset Griffon Vendeen
Pharaoh Hounds
Rhodesian Ridgebacks
Salukis
Scottish Deerhounds
Whippets

TOY GROUP
Affenpinschers
Brussels Griffons
Chihuahuas
Chinese Crested
English Toy Spaniels
Italian Greyhounds
Japanese Chin
Maltese
Manchester Terriers
Miniature Pinschers
Papillons
Pekingese
Pomeranians
Poodles
Pugs
Shih Tzu
Silky Terriers
Yorkshire Terriers

NON-SPORTING GROUP
Bichons Frises
Boston Terriers
Bulldogs
Chow Chow
Dalmatians
Finnish Spitz
French Bulldogs
Keeshonden
Lhasa Apsos

Poodles (Miniature)
Poodles (Standard)
Schipperkes
Tibetan Spaniels
Tibetan Terriers

HERDING GROUP

Australian Cattle Dogs
Bearded Collies
Belgian Malinois
Belgian Sheepdogs
Belgian Tervuren
Bouviers des Flandres
Briards
Collies
German Shepherd Dogs
Old English Sheepdogs
Pulik
Shetland Sheepdogs
Welsh Corgis (Cardigan)
Welsh Corgis (Pembroke)

WORKING GROUP

Akitas
Alaskan Malamutes
Bernese Mountain Dogs
Boxers
Bullmastiffs
Doberman Pinschers
Giant Schnauzers
Great Danes
Great Pyrenees
Komondorok
Kuvaszok
Mastiffs
Newfoundlands
Portuguese Water Dogs
Rottweilers
St. Bernards
Samoyeds
Siberian Huskies
Standard Schnauzers

TERRIER GROUP

Airedales
American Staffordshire Terriers
Australian Terriers
Bedlington Terriers
Border Terriers
Bull Terriers
Cairn Terriers
Dandie Dinmont Terriers
Fox Terriers (Smooth)
Fox Terriers (Wire)
Irish Terriers
Kerry Blue Terriers
Lakeland Terriers
Manchester Terriers (Standard)
Miniature Schnauzers
Norfolk Terriers
Norwich Terriers
Scottish Terriers
Sealyham Terriers
Skye Terriers
Soft-coated Wheaten Terriers
Staffordshire Bull Terriers
Welsh Terriers
West Highland White Terriers

MISCELLANEOUS CLASSES

(Not eligible for group competition)

Australian Kelpie
Border Collie
Canaan Dog
Cavalier King Charles Spaniel
Chinese Shar-Pei
Greater Swiss Mountain Dog
Miniature Bull Terrier
Spinoni Italiani

Appendix III

FOREIGN DOG REGISTRIES
The following organizations can be contacted for information on international competitions.

AUSTRIA
Osterreichischer Kynologenverband
Johann Teufel — Gasse 8
A-1238 Vienna, Austria

BELGIUM
Societe Royale Saint-Hubert
Avenue de l'Armee 25
B-1040 Brussels, Belgium

BERMUDA
The Bermuda Kennel Club
P.O. Box HM 1455
Hamilton, Bermuda HM FX

CANADA
The Canadian Kennel Club
100-89 Skyway Avenue
Etobicoke, Ontario
M9W 6R4, Canada

COLOMBIA
Associacion "Club Canino
    Colombiano"
Aparatedo Aereo 102268
Bogota, D.E.
Colombia

CZECHOSLOVAKIA
Cynological Federation of CSSR
Opletalova 29
11631 Praha 1
Czechoslovakia

DENMARK
Dansk Kennel Club
Parkvej 1
DK-2680 Solrod Strand
Denmark

FINLAND
Finska Kennelklubben r.y.
Kamreerintie 8
02770 Espoo, Finland

FRANCE
Societe Centrale Canine
215, Rue St. Denis-75093
Paris Cedex 02
France

HOLLAND
Raad Van Beheer op Kynologisch
    Gebied in Nederland
Emmalaan 16-18
Postbus 5901
1007 AX Amsterdam-Z
The Netherlands

HUNGARY
Magyar Ebtenyesztok Orszagos
    Egyesulete
Fadrusz utca 11/a
H-114 Budapest XL
Hungary

IRELAND (Not including Northern
    Ireland)
The Irish Kennel Club
Unit 36
Greenmount Office Park
Dublin 6, Ireland

ITALY
Ente Nazionale Della Cinofilia Italiana
    (ENCI)
Viale Premuda, 21
20129 Milan, Italy

MEXICO
Federacion Canofila Mexicana A.C.
Zapotecas No. 29
Talpan, C.P. 14430
Mexico, D.F., Mexico

MONACO
Societe Canine de Monaco
Avenue d'Ostende
Palais des Congres
Monte Carlo, Monaco

NEW ZEALAND
The New Zealand Kennel Club (Inc.)
Private Bag
Porirua
New Zealand

NORWAY
Norsk Kennel Club
Nils Hansens vei 20
Box 163 — Bryn
0611 Oslo 6
Norway

PANAMA
Club Canino de Panama
Apartado 6-4791
El Dorado, Panama
Republic of Panama

PHILIPPINES
The Philippine Canine Club, Inc.
P.O. Box 649
Greenhills Post Office
1502 San Juan
Metro Manila, Philippines

PORTUGAL
Clube Portuguese de Canicultura
Praca D. Joao Da Camara, 4,3.0-Esq.
Lisbon 2, Portugal

SINGAPORE
The Singapore Kennel Club
170, Upper Bukit Timah Road, #12-02
Singapore 2158, Singapore

SOUTH AFRICA
The Kennel Union of Southern Africa
P.O. Box 2659
Cape Town 8000
Republic of South Africa

SWEDEN
Svenska Kennelklubben
Box 11043
161 11 Bromma, Sweden

SWITZERLAND
Stammbuchsekretariat der SKG
Postfach 8363
3001 Bern
Switzerland

UNITED KINGDOM (Including
    Northern Ireland)
The Kennel Club
1-5 Clarges Street
Piccadilly, London
W1Y 8AB, England

VENEZUELA
Federacion Canina Venezuela
Apartado 88665
Caracas 1080-A, Venezuela

**Federation Cynologique
    Internationale**
14 Rueheopold 2
6530 Thuin
Belgium
The Federation is the governing body
    for all European shows.

Index